Oregon Revolutionary War Memorial

Volume 1
2018

www.ORWM.org

Copyright ©2017 Michael Tieman. All Rights reserved. No part of this publication may be reproduced, stored in a retrieval system, or transmitted in any way, or by any means, electronic, mechanical, photocopying, recording, or otherwise, without the prior written permission of the copyright holder.

ISBN-13: 978-0-9910977-4-6

Design by Michael L. Tieman, Artists Gallerie, LLC

Printed in the United States

Published by Michael Tieman Publishing
15724 SW Flagstone Dr.
Beaverton, OR 97007, United States
www.artistsgallerie.com

First Edition Volume 1   2018

In Memory Of

Sons of the American Revolution
Compatriot Grier Ingebretsen
1942 - 2017
who was taken from us suddenly
by cancer.

This Memorial was his idea,
his passion, his spirit and his soul.
Unfortunately, he did not see it completed.

Rest in Peace our friend and fellow Compatriot.
We have the watch.

Contents

Foreword	6
Our Partners	7
The Journey	11
Patriot Muster Roll	17
A	18
B	21
C	34
D	44
E	50
F	52
G	56
H	63
I	72
J	73
K	74
L	76

M	81
N	91
O	92
P	93
Q	104
R	104
S	111
T	121
U	125
V	126
Y	136
Z	136
Name Index	139

Foreword

"To construct a living, interactive memorial in the Beaverton Veterans Memorial Park to HONOR our forefathers who served or assisted the colonies during the American Revolutionary War and to EDUCATE our children and future generations about the American Revolution and the price and responsibilities of FREEDOM."

This is a labor of love and commitment by our Partners and many dedicated individuals, schools, organizations and government agencies.

These are the people who are charged with the research, and digging through tons of records to gather the data to not only be placed on the physical memorial, but to be placed in one database online for all to read any time and from anywhere in the world.

We cannot do this enourmous project without them.

Our eternal thanks.

Our Partners

OREGON SOCIETY SONS OF THE AMERICAN REVOLUTION

The SAR is a patriotic, historical, and educational non-profit corporation, that seeks to maintain and extend the institutions of American freedom, an appreciation for true patriotism, a respect for our national symbols, the value of American citizenship, and the unifying force of "E Pluribus Unum".

AMERICAN LEGION BEAVERTON POST #124

Our American Legion Post has been welcoming VETERANS from all branches of our Armed Forces. Today, we continue to welcome all military personnel serving our country. Joining our Post enables you to continue serving your God, Country and Community Our mission is to implement the goals, aspirations, dreams, peace and blessings for our country, friends and families embodied in our preamble.

CITY OF BEAVERTON

The City of Beaverton is located seven miles west of Portland, Oregon, in the Tualatin River Valley, encompasses 19.6 square miles, and is home to more than 95,000 residents. The city is Oregon's sixth largest city and the second-largest incorporated city in Washington County.

BEAVERTON SCHOOL DISTRICT

The unified Beaverton School District was founded in July 1960. Today, we educate more than 40,000 students in 51 schools. We are the third-largest school district in Oregon. Beaverton schools are dedicated to providing outstanding, challenging educational opportunities that prepare all students to be college and career ready.

BEAVERTON CITY LIBRARY

The Beaverton City Library, the second busiest library in the state, serves a population of approximately 142,000 (the population of Beaverton plus a portion of the unincorporated residents of Washington County). Each month over 84,000 people visit the Library to check out nearly 300,000 items. The total annual circulation exceeds 3.3 million items. The Library has two facilities each open seven days per week.

OREGON SOCIETY DAUGHTERS OF THE AMERICAN REVOLUTION

The DAR, founded in 1890 and headquartered in Washington, D.C., is a non-profit, non-political volunteer women's service organization dedicated to promoting patriotism, preserving American history, and securing America's future through better education for children.

The Journey

"To construct a living, interactive memorial in Beaverton Veterans Memorial Park to HONOR our forefathers who served or assisted the colonies during the American Revolutionary War and to EDUCATE our children and the world about the revolution and the price and responsibilities of FREEDOM."

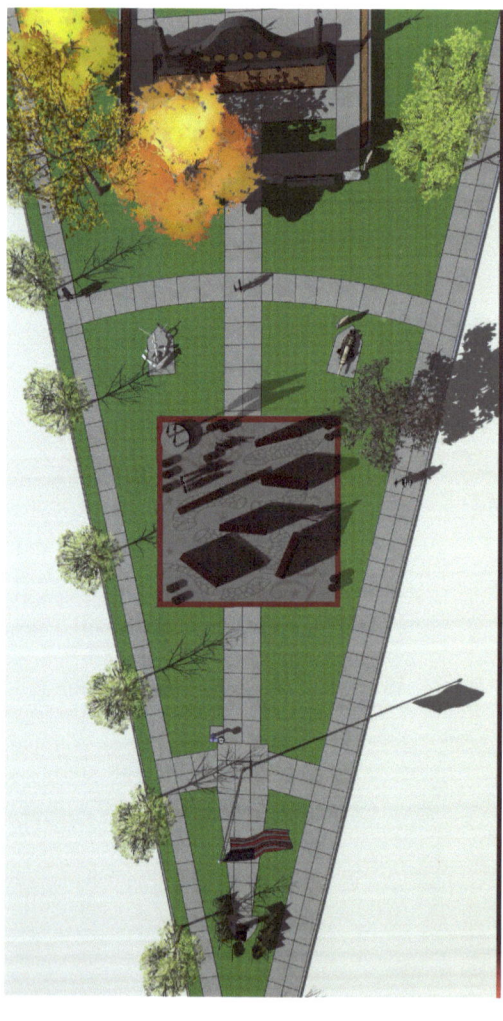

A PHYSICAL MEMORIAL WITH AN INTERACTIVE LIBRARY

As you stand in front of the Oregon Revolutionary War Memorial one is struck by the magnitude of the story scribed on the walls but also that this is only a small amount compared to the interactive library supporting it.

The memorial was first conceived by Compatriot Grier Ingebretsen, Lewis & Clark Chapter, Oregon Sons of the American Revolution to remember Patriot ancestors who fought for their freedom, and to educate our children and future generations about the price of that freedom. Also, in the Beaverton Memorial Park the one war not represented was the first American struggle, the American Revolutionary War.

As the design evolved, the concept grew from just another "Memorial Wall" to a living, breathing interactive memorial encompassing Patriotic, Historical, and Educational values.

Now the vision congealed into a two-part memorial. The very visible first part is of course the physical memorial in the park. Comprising of six walls arranged in the shape of the snake on one of the nation's first flags ... Join, or Die. The second part is the living information with the ability to update, change and improve and stored for retrieval by anyone, anywhere at any time.

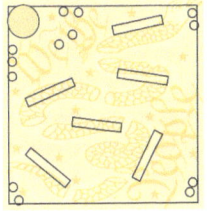

How then does this work?

Strolling around the physical memorial, etched on the sides of the walls is historical and patriotic images and information.

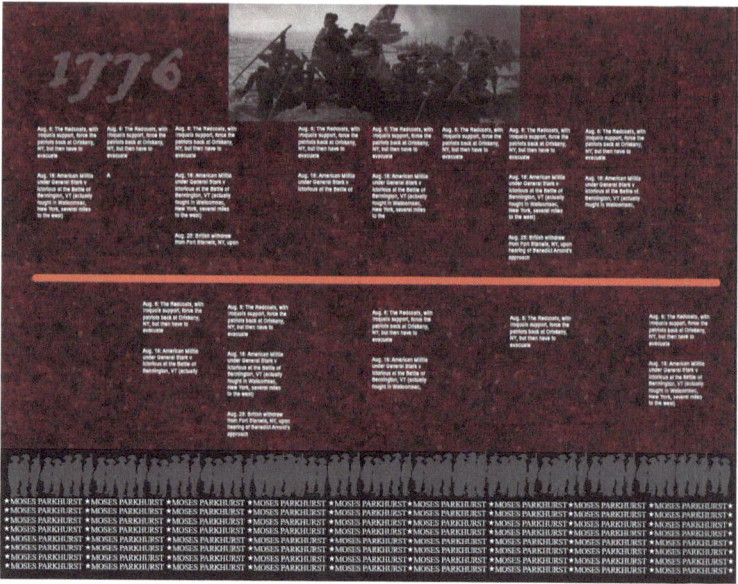

Along the bottom of the walls are the names of some of the Patriots who sacrificed their lives and fortunes in the War and whose descendants are members of the Oregon Sons of the American Revolution and the Oregon Daughters of the American Revolution.

Next to the list is a QR code that when you scan it on your mobile device, it takes you to a webpage that has the biographies of those Patriots. It also has links to DAR and SAR databases where you can get more information, and see if maybe you are related to a Patriot.

Sections of journal pages written by the men who were fighting at Valley Forge, the Hudson River area and Yorktown as an example. The QR codes link to more journals, and to Historical and Genealogical society libraries not only in Oregon, but across the United States.

A graphic yearly time line from before the war years to 1790 when the Constitution was finally ratified by Rhode Island. The information above the time line are the dates of some of the major battles fought, and the information below the time line are major events in the lives of the people that influenced the battles. Scan the QR codes to get to more information and links on the events.

Images and writings of everyday life of the colonists; clothes, toys, what they ate and what their homes and business looked like. QR codes again take you to more information and links, while you are still standing in front of the memorial in Beaverton.

Let's not forget about those Patriots. Life size images carved in the stone of a Minuteman, a Militia and a Continental soldier with descriptions of who they were and how they dressed. Then the flags

they fought and died under both on, land, and sea, flying in the breeze adding color and life to the memorial.

What a project! The scope is too large for one group or organization to handle and keep updated for years.

This is a labor of love and commitment by many dedicated individuals, organizations, schools and government agencies. These are the people who are charged with the research, and the digging through the tons of records to gather the data.

Our Partners are the national and state societies and local chapters of the SAR and DAR, American Legion, Historical societies, Genealogical societies, libraries, government agencies, schools and you.

This is a long-term project, funding and building the memorial in the park will take time, and gathering and updating the information will take decades, but together we can all make this happen.

Michael L. Tieman
2018

Patriot Muster Roll

A

ABBOTT, JOSEPH
New Jersey, Oregon DAR Daughter

ABBOTT, WILLIAM
New Hampshire, Oregon DAR Daughter

ADAMS, GILBERT
New York, Oregon DAR Daughter

ADAMS, JOEL, PVT.
Massachusetts, Oregon DAR Daughter

ADAMS, JOHN
Massachusetts, SAR Compatriot Mark Robertson, Oregon DAR Daughter

ADAMS, JOHN
Pennsylvania, Oregon DAR Daughter

ADAMS, MATHEW
New Jersey, Oregon DAR Daughter

ADAMS, OLIVER
Massachusetts, Oregon DAR Daughter

ADAMS, SAMUEL
Connecticut, Oregon DAR Daughter

ADSIT, BENJAMIN, PVT.
New York, Oregon DAR Daughter

ALBRIGHT, BERNARD, PVT.
Pennsylvania, Oregon DAR Daughter

ALDEN, SILAS, LT.
Massachusetts, Oregon DAR Daughter

ALEXANDER, JAMES
Pennsylvania, North Carolina, Oregon DAR Daughter

ALEXANDER, WILLIAM, LT.
Maryland, Oregon DAR Daughter

ALLEN, ANANIAS
New Jersey, Oregon DAR Daughter

ALLEN, ISHAM, PVT.
Virginia, Oregon DAR Daughter

ALLEN, JOB, CAPT.
New Jersey, Oregon DAR Daughter

ALLEN, JOHN, PVT.
Connecticut, Oregon DAR Daughter

ALLEN, MALCUM
Virginia, Oregon DAR Daughter

ALLIS, MOSES, SGT.
Massachusetts, Oregon DAR Daughter

ALSPACH, HENRY
Pennsylvania, Oregon DAR Daughter

ALSTON, JOSEPH JOHN
North Carolina, Oregon DAR Daughter

ALSTON, WILLIS WILSON, COL.
North Carolina, Oregon DAR Daughter

ALSTOTT, JOHN
Pennsylvania, Oregon DAR Daughter

ALTMAN, JOHN PETER
Pennsylvania, Oregon DAR Daughter

AMMIDOWN, PHILIP
Oregon DAR Daughter

ANDERSON, ABSOLOM, LT.
Maryland, Oregon DAR Daughter

ANDERSON, BENJAMIN
Virginia, Oregon DAR Daughter

ANDERSON, ELIJAH
North Carolina, Oregon DAR Daughter

ANDERSON, JOSEPH
Massachusetts, New York, Oregon DAR Daughter

ANDERSON, WILLIAM CLARK, PVT.
Maryland, Oregon DAR Daughter

ANDREWS, ROBERT
Pennsylvania, Oregon DAR Daughter

ANDREWS, WILLIAM,
North Carolina, Oregon DAR Daughter

ANTES, JOHN HENRY, SR.
Oregon DAR Daughter

APP, MICHAEL, PVT.
Pennsylvania, Oregon DAR Daughter

APPLEBY, JAMES
SAR Compatriot Gordon Fultz

APPLEGATE, DANIEL, FIFER & DRUMMER
New Jersey, Oregon DAR Daughter

ARENDALL, NATHAN, PVT.
New Hampshire, SAR Compatriot Ken Betterton, Oregon DAR Daughter

ARMSTRONG, JOSHUA, PVT.
Pennsylvania, Oregon DAR Daughter

ARTHUR, JOHN
Pennsylvania, Oregon DAR Daughter

ASHCRAFT, ICHABOD
Pennsylvania, Oregon DAR Daughter

ASHLEY, WILLIAM, SGT.
Vermont, Oregon DAR Daughter

ASHMEAD, JOHN
Pennsylvania, Oregon DAR Daughter

ATKINSON, JOHN, PVT.
Virginia, Oregon DAR Daughter

ATWOOD, ELISHA
Connecticut, Oregon DAR Daughter

ATWOOD, ZACCHEUS
Massachusetts, Oregon DAR Daughter

AUSTIN, DAVID, PVT.
Rhode Island, Oregon DAR Daughter

AUSTIN, DAVID, SR.
Connecticut, Oregon DAR Daughter

AUSTIN, SILAS
Rhode Island, Oregon DAR Daughter

B

BABCOCK, RUEBEN, PVT.
Massachusetts, Oregon DAR Daughter

BAGER, JOHN GEORGE, REV.
Pennsylvania, Oregon DAR Daughter

BAGLEY, HARMON
Rhode Island, Oregon DAR Daughter

BAILEY, RICHARD
Oregon DAR Daughter

BAILEY, RICHARD, SR.
Rhode Island, Oregon DAR Daughter

BAILEY, SAMUEL
SAR Compatriot Donald Robinson

BAKER, BENAJAH, PVT.
Rhode Island DAR Daughter Merilee Mulvey, Oregon DAR Daughter
   Born in 1747 in East Greenwich, Kent County, Rhode Island from a family of farmers. He married Mary Manchester and they raised a family of 11 children.
   Benajah served as a private with men from Scituate and Exeter, Rhode Island during the Revolutionary War. After

the war, Benajah and his family migrated northeast through Massachusetts and Vermont into Canada, finally settling around Stanbridge Twp. in Missisquoi County, Quebec, Canada.

BAKER, DAVID
Virginia, Oregon DAR Daughter

BAKER, JOSEPH
Massachusetts, Oregon DAR Daughter

BAKER, MOSES, JR.
North Carolina, Oregon DAR Daughter

BAKER, SAMUEL
Massachusetts, Oregon DAR Daughter

BALCH, BENJAMIN
Massachusetts, Oregon DAR Daughter

BALDWIN, THOMAS
Virginia, Oregon DAR Daughter

BALL, WILLIAM, LT.
Virginia, Oregon DAR Daughter

BALLENGER, JAMES
SAR Compatriot George Lanning

BANKS, JAMES
Pennsylvania, Oregon DAR Daughter

BANKS, JOSHUA
Connecticut, Oregon DAR Daughter

BANKS, THOMAS
North Carolina, Oregon DAR Daughter

BANNER, CASPER
Virginia, Oregon DAR Daughter

BARKLEY, JACOB, PVT.
Pennsylvania, SAR Compatriot George Degner

BARNETT, PHILIP
DAR Daughter Belle Passi Chapter

BARNETT, ROBERT
Virginia, Oregon DAR Daughter

BARNUM, ABIJAH
Connecticut, Oregon DAR Daughter

BARRETT, JONATHAN, PVT.
Massachusetts, Oregon DAR Daughter

BARTLET, JOSIAH, COL.
Signer of Declaration of Independence, New Hampshire, Oregon DAR Daughter

BARTLETT, SUSANNAH DAVIS
Virginia, Oregon DAR Daughter

BARTLETT, THOMAS
Virginia, Oregon DAR Daughter

BARTON, ELISHA
Pennsylvania, Oregon DAR Daughter

BARWICK, WILLIAM
North Carolina, Oregon DAR Daughter

BASHAM, OBEDIAH, PVT.
Virginia, Oregon DAR Daughter

BASSETT, JOTHAM, PVT.
Massachusetts, DAR Daughter Evelyn Laughman

BASSETT, RUFUS, SGT.
Massachusetts, Vermont, Oregon DAR Daughter

BATCHELLER/BATCHELDER, BENJAMIN, PVT.
Massachusetts, Vermont, Oregon DAR Daughter

BATHHURST, LAWRENCE
Pennsylvania, Oregon DAR Daughter

BAXTER, PETTIE
New York, Oregon DAR Daughter

BAYARD, STEPHEN
Maryland, Oregon DAR Daughter

BEAL, JOSEPH
 DAR Daughter Sue Glenn

BEAL, JOSHUA, PVT.
 Massachusetts, Oregon DAR Daughter

BEALLE, BENJAMIN, SR.
 Massachusetts, Oregon DAR Daughter

BEAM, HENRY
 Pennsylvania, Oregon DAR Daughter

BEAMAN, ELIJAH, LT.
 Vermont, Oregon DAR Daughter

BEAN, WILLIAM
 North Carolina, Oregon DAR Daughter

BEATTY, JOHN
 Pennsylvania, Oregon DAR Daughter

BECKETT, HUMPHREY
 Virginia, Oregon DAR Daughter

BEDIENT, MORDECAI, PVT.
 Connecticut, Oregon DAR Daughter

BEDINGER, PETER
 Virginia, Oregon DAR Daughter

BEER, ROBERT
 SAR Compatriot Richard Scott

BEERS, JOEL, PVT.
 Webb's Reg. & Invalid Corps., 1778-1783, SAR Compatriot Arlen Clark

BELEW, SOLOMON, PVT.
 Virginia, Oregon DAR Daughter

BELL, ROBERT
 North Carolina, Oregon DAR Daughter

BELL, THOMAS, PVT.
 North Carolina, Oregon DAR Daughter

BELLOWS, THOMAS
    8th Reg. of Connecticut. SAR Compatriots Johnny Alexander, Tyler McClintock

BENEDICT, SAMUEL, PVT.
    Connecticut, Oregon DAR Daughter

BENNETT, BATCHELOR, CPL.
    Massachusetts, Oregon DAR Daughter

BENNETT, ISAAC
    Connecticut, Oregon DAR Daughter

BENNETT, JOSHUA, JR.
    Connecticut, Oregon DAR Daughter

BENSON, PETER, PVT.
    Massachusetts, Oregon DAR Daughter

BENSON, STEPHEN, CPL.
    Massachusetts, Oregon DAR Daughter

BENT, DAVID
    DAR Daughter Belle Passi Chapter

BERTRAM, WILLIAM
    North Carolina, Oregon DAR Daughter

BESS, PETER
    North Carolina, Oregon DAR Daughter

BETTY, GEORGE
    North Carolina, Oregon DAR Daughter

BIBLE, JOHN ADAM
    Virginia, Oregon DAR Daughter

BICKEL, PETER
    Pennsylvania, Oregon DAR Daughter

BICKNELL, JOHN
    Massachusetts, Oregon DAR Daughter

BIERY, HENRY
    Pennsylvania, Oregon DAR Daughter

BIERY, MICHAEL, NONCOM.
Pennsylvania, Oregon DAR Daughter

BIGGS, ROBERT
DAR Daughter Belle Passi Chapter

BILLINGS, THADDEUS
DAR Daughter Belle Passi Chapter

BINGHAM, JONATHON
New Hampshire, Oregon DAR Daughter

BISHOP, WILLIAM, PVT.
Rhode Island, Oregon DAR Daughter

BLACKBURN, THOMAS
Pennsylvania, Oregon DAR Daughter

BLAIR, BRICE
Pennsylvania, Oregon DAR Daughter

BLANCHARD, DANIEL
DAR Daughter Sue Glenn

BLANCHARD, DANIEL, SR., PVT.
Massachusetts, Oregon DAR Daughter

BLAND, THOMAS
Virginia, Oregon DAR Daughter

BLARE, JAMES
Virginia, Oregon DAR Daughter

BLASDEL, JACOB
New Hampshire, Oregon DAR Daughter

BLISS, JAMES
Connecticut, Oregon DAR Daughter

BLISS, NATHAN, PVT.
Massachusetts, Oregon DAR Daughter

BLOOD, SIMON, PVT.
Massachusetts, Oregon DAR Daughter

BLOOMER, REUBEN, ENS.
   Vermont, Oregon DAR Daughter

BLOUNT, WALTER
   Connecticut, Oregon DAR Daughter

BLUE, JOHN, JR., PVT.
   Virginia, Oregon DAR Daughter

BOATWRIGHT, JAMES
   Virginia, Oregon DAR Daughter

BOCKOVEN, GEORGE, LT.
   New Jersey, Oregon DAR Daughter

BOLLING (BOWLING), JARRETT, PVT.
   Virginia, Oregon DAR Daughter

BOMBERGER, JOHN, PVT.
   Lancaster Co. Pennsylvania Militia, 1778-1785,
   SAR Compatriot Arlen Clark, Oregon DAR Daughter

BOONE, EDWARD
   Juror; Road Viewer, Defender of the Fort North Carolina and Virginia, SAR Compatriot Teddy Mills
   Birth: 30 Nov 1740 in Pennsylvania Death: 6 Oct 1780 at Blue Licks, Kentucky Edward Boone looked like his older brother, Daniel. Edward and Daniel married sisters, Martha and Rebecca Bryan, but the brothers' similarities may have ended there. While Daniel was off exploring the woods and cutting new trails, Edward stayed home with his family in Wilkes County, North Carolina.
   Edward and Martha had six children, Charity b. 1760, Jane b. 1762, Mary b. 1764, George b. 1767, Joseph b. 1768, and Sarah b. 1771. It was during these years until 1779 that Edward was a community and church leader in NC. He served on juries, was a road surveyor, a tax collector, and a constable.
   Although for many years the Boones had been Quakers, Edward was baptized in the Mulberry Fields Branch of the Dutchman Creek Baptist Church, Jan. 22, 1774. It was said he loved to sing. He served his church as a deacon and a clerk. He was "called Ned by his family and friends," and Edward Boone "was "a peace man."
   On September 9, 1779, Edward entered 200 acres of

land "lying on Beavers Creek adjoining to Thos. Henderson, beginning and running so as to include his improvements."

Only about a month later, in October 1779 he made that fateful decision to move his family to Kentucky with Daniel who was leading a large party of family members there for the promise of free land.

Edward and Martha hastily gathered their family and all their belongings and joined the other family members from NC. It was said, "Edward Boone packed 22 horses in addition to the ones the family rode."

They traveled through the Cumberland Gap, up the Wilderness Trail, and settled at Boone Station not far from Fort Boonesborough, arriving December 22, 1779. Fifteen other family members shared the station.

The Virginia government had authority to issue land certificates for 400 acres where a settler's right of occupation was established. Hearings began October 13, 1779. If the settlers in North Carolina were to receive valid land claims, it was imperative that they return to Kentucky and submit their claim. Thus a large group from North Carolina set out for Kentucky in October 1779. The exodus was described by one man as like an army movement, and when they camped for the night, would be in a string a half-mile long.

After meeting with the Virginia Land Commission, Daniel Boone, his brother, Squire and his son, Israel, established their claims and were granted lands by the commission.

Edward apparently did not receive any land. He continued living at Boone Station, caring for his family and hunting for food to also share with the Bryan family at Bryan Station. Joseph Bryan was his father-in-law and one of the founders of Bryan Station.

Because the area of Boone Station was so remote and traveling to the county seat was dangerous at best, Edward was one of the signers on May 1, 1780 of Petition #12 that resulted in splitting Kentucky County, Virginia, into 3 counties: Jefferson, Fayette, and Lincoln. Part of the petition reads, "That the Militia Inhabitants of the north side of Kaintucky amount to about 400 with 11 fortified posts ... that the nearest settlement to the Courthouse is at least 40 miles and the farthest about 70 miles ... that the River Kentucky is rendered impassable half the year by high waters and is ever inconvenient and dangerous ..." The petition was approved by the Virginia Legislature.

Edward had lived in Kentucky less than a year when on October 6, 1780, he was killed by Indians (probably Shawnee) while he and Daniel were returning from the Blue Licks to make salt and do a little hunting.

They stopped along a stream in Bourbon County to rest and let their horses drink. Edward sat down by the stream near an old Buckeye tree and was cracking nuts, while Daniel went off into the woods in pursuit of game.

Indians lurking nearby shot and killed Edward, but Daniel managed to escape. He ran all the way on foot to Boone Station (about 40 miles) where they were all living at the time. The next morning Daniel and a party of men in the area went in search of Edward's killers. They did not find the Indians, but found and buried Edward near that old Buckeye tree.

Today in that very spot stands an old Buckeye tree, perhaps grown from a seedling of the original tree. The creek was afterward named Boone Creek in honor of Edward's death there. As Jeff Johnson, a descendant of Edward Boone, says of the death site, "the bubbling sounds of the stream running over the rocks are probably the last sounds Edward heard as he lay dying."

Ned's daughter, Sarah Boone Hunter, in a letter to Draper, said "My father was killed 40 miles from the Station. He was stabbed in 7 places; his fingers were horribly cut with the Indian's knives. He was scalped, and part of his clothing was taken off; I think his coat and pantaloons."

Although still a young woman, Martha never remarried and remained in Kentucky until her death.

BOONE, JOSIAH, SR.
Virginia, Oregon DAR Daughter

BOONE, REBECCA BRYAN
Virginia, Oregon DAR Daughter

BOONE, SQUIRE, SGT.
South Carolina, Oregon DAR Daughter

BOSTWICH, BENJAMIN
Connecticut, Oregon DAR Daughter

BOSWORTH, CONSTANT
Massachusetts, Oregon DAR Daughter

BOSWORTH, NATHANIEL, CPL.
  Vermont, Oregon DAR Daughter

BOTTS, JOHN
  Virginia, Oregon DAR Daughter

BOURNE, STEPHEN, SR.
  Virginia, Oregon DAR Daughter

BOWEN, HENRY
  Virginia, Oregon DAR Daughter

BOWEN, LILY MCILHANEY
  Virginia, Oregon DAR Daughter

BOWLSBY, DANIEL
  New Jersey, Oregon DAR Daughter

BOWLSBY, SAMUEL, PVT.
  New Jersey, Oregon DAR Daughter

BOWMAN, PHILIP
  DAR Daughter Belle Passi Chapter

BOWSER, JOHN
  Pennsylvania, Oregon DAR Daughter

BOYD, JAMES
  DAR Daughter Belle Passi Chapter

BOYDEN, JOHN
  Massachusetts, Oregon DAR Daughter

BOYER, CASPER
  Maryland, Oregon DAR Daughter

BOYNTON, AMOS
  New Hampshire, Oregon DAR Daughter

BOZARTH, JOSEPH
  Virginia, Oregon DAR Daughter

BRACKEN, ISAAC
  DAR Daughter Patti Waitman-Ingebretsen

BRADBURY, BENJAMIN, SGT.
   Massachusetts, Oregon DAR Daughter

BRADISH, DANIEL
   DAR Daughter Belle Passi Chapter

BRADLEY, ELISHA
   Vermont, Oregon DAR Daughter

BRANCH, EDWARD
   Virginia, Oregon DAR Daughter

BREED, OLIVER
   SAR Compatriot John Spiegel

BRENTON, JAMES
   Virginia, Oregon DAR Daughter

BRICKER, JOHN, JR., CPL.
   Massachusetts, Oregon DAR Daughter

BRIDGFORTH, BENJAMIN
   Virginia, Oregon DAR Daughter

BRIDGFORTH, JAMES
   Virginia, Oregon DAR Daughter

BRIDGHAM, JOHN, SR., CAPT.
   Massachusetts, Oregon DAR Daughter

BRIGGS, OWEN
   Massachusetts, Connecticut, Oregon DAR Daughter

BRIGHAM, ASA, MAJ.
   New Hampshire, Oregon DAR Daughter

BRISCOE, HENRY, PVT.
   Maryland, Oregon DAR Daughter

BRITTON, PENDLETON, PVT.
   Massachusetts, Oregon DAR Daughter

BROADDUS, THOMAS
   Virginia, Oregon DAR Daughter

BROCK, JESSE
North Carolina, Oregon DAR Daughter

BROCKWAY, EBENEZER
Connecticut, Oregon DAR Daughter

BROKAW, ISAAC
SAR Compatriot Willis Meisenheimer

BROOKHART/BURKHEART, PHILIP
SAR Compatriot Kenneth Brookhart

BROOKS, WILLIAM
DAR Daughter Belle Passi Chapter

BROUGH, HERMANUS, SR.
Pennsylvania, Oregon DAR Daughter

BROWN, AMOS, SGT.
Massachusetts, Oregon DAR Daughter

BROWN, EPHRAIM
Massachusetts, Oregon DAR Daughter

BROWN, HEZEKIAH
Virginia, Oregon DAR Daughter

BROWN, JOSEPH
Virginia, Oregon DAR Daughter

BROWN, KNIGHT, PVT.
Massachusetts, DAR Daughter Sue Glenn

BROWN, LEWIS
Virginia, Oregon DAR Daughter

BROWN, RUFUS
Massachusetts, Oregon DAR Daughter

BROWN, SAMUEL
Massachusetts, Oregon DAR Daughter

BROWN, THOMAS
Virginia, Oregon DAR Daughter

BRUCE, JOHN, SGT.
Virginia, Oregon DAR Daughter

BUCHANAN, GEORGE
Pennsylvania, Oregon DAR Daughter

BUCHANAN, ROBERT, CAPT.
Virginia, Oregon DAR Daughter

BUCKLIN, JOHN
Rhode Island, Oregon DAR Daughter

BUCKNER, WILLIAM
Virginia, Oregon DAR Daughter

BUELL, JEDEDIAH, JR.
Connecticut, Oregon DAR Daughter

BULL, AMBROSE
SAR Compatriot Samuel Waddell

BURCHAM, JOHN, SR.
North Carolina, Oregon DAR Daughter

BURKHALTER, JOHN PETER, JR., ENS.
Pennsylvania, Oregon DAR Daughter

BURKHALTER, PETER, SR., LTCOL.
Pennsylvania, Oregon DAR Daughter

BURKHART, GEORGE
Maryland, Oregon DAR Daughter

BURNHAM, AMMI
Massachusetts, Oregon DAR Daughter

BURNS, WILLIAM, PVT.
Virginia, North Carolina, Oregon DAR Daughter

BUSH, JAMES
Pennsylvania, Oregon DAR Daughter

BUSHNELL, GIDEON, PVT.
Oregon DAR Daughter

BUSHNELL, JOHN HANDLEY
Connecticut, Oregon DAR Daughter

BUTCHER, SAMUEL, LT.
Virginia, DAR Daughter Belle Passi Chapter

BUTLER, JOSEPH
Connecticut, Oregon DAR Daughter

BUTTS, SHERABIAH, CAPT.
Connecticut, Oregon DAR Daughter

BUTZ, JOHN
Pennsylvania, Oregon DAR Daughter

BUZBEE, JACOB, PVT.
South Carolina, Oregon DAR Daughter

BYAM, SAMUEL, PVT.
DAR Daughter Janice Gadway Gardner

C

CABLE, ABRAHAM
Pennsylvania, Oregon DAR Daughter

CADY, STODARD
SAR Compatriot Stephen Price

CAIN, DANIEL, PVT.
Massachusetts, DAR Daughter Sue Glenn

CALDWELL, ROBERT
Virginia, Oregon DAR Daughter

CALHOUN, REBECCA FLORIDE PICKENS
South Carolina, Oregon DAR Daughter

CALKINS, JOHN
Connecticut, Oregon DAR Daughter

CALLAWAY, THOMAS, SR.
North Carolina, Oregon DAR Daughter

CALLENDER, JOHN, LT.
New York, Oregon DAR Daughter

CAMP, JOB
Connecticut, Oregon DAR Daughter

CAMPBELL, ARCHIBALD
Virginia Oregon DAR Daughter

CAMPBELL, CHARLES, PVT.
Virginia Oregon DAR Daughter

CAMPBELL, JAMES
Virginia Oregon DAR Daughter

CAMPBELL, JAMES
Massachusetts, Oregon DAR Daughter

CAMPBELL, MCDONALD
New Jersey, Oregon DAR Daughter

CAMPBELL, WILLIAM, CPL.
Massachusetts, Oregon DAR Daughter

CAMPFIELD, WILLIAM
New Jersey, Oregon DAR Daughter

CANFIELD, DANIEL
New York, Oregon DAR Daughter

CANNON, JAMES
South Carolina, Oregon DAR Daughter

CANNON, SAMUEL
South Carolina, Oregon DAR Daughter

CARPENTER, ADAM, PVT.
Virginia, Oregon DAR Daughter

CARPENTER, ANN SHUTLEY
Virginia, Oregon DAR Daughter

CARPENTER, GEORGE, SR., PVT.
Virginia, Oregon DAR Daughter

CARPENTER, JOHN, PVT.
Pennsylvania, Oregon DAR Daughter

CARPENTER, WILLIAM
Massachusetts, Oregon DAR Daughter

CARR, GIDEON
Virginia, Oregon DAR Daughter

CARR, JOHN
Virginia, Oregon DAR Daughter

CARR, JOHN FENDELL
Virginia, Oregon DAR Daughter

CARROLL, WILLIAM
DAR Daughter Belle Passi Chapter

CARTER, GEORGE
South Carolina, Georgia, Oregon DAR Daughter

CARTER, JOHN B.
Virginia, Oregon DAR Daughter

CARTER, LEVI
DAR Daughter Belle Passi Chapter

CARTER, PETER
Virginia, Oregon DAR Daughter

CARTER, SAMUEL
SAR Compatriots William Murray, Peter Murray

CARTWRIGHT, PETER
Virginia, Oregon DAR Daughter

CASTOR, FREDERICK, LT.
Pennsylvania, Oregon DAR Daughter

CAVE, RICHARD, REV.
Virginia, Oregon DAR Daughter

CHAFFEE, EZRA, CAPT.
Connecticut, Vermont, Oregon DAR Daughter

CHAFFIN, EPHRAIM, PVT.
Massachusetts, Oregon DAR Daughter

CHAIN, WILLIAM
Pennsylvania, Oregon DAR Daughter

CHALFANT, SOLOMON, PVT.
Virginia, Oregon DAR Daughter

CHAMBERLAIN, NATHANIEL
Massachusetts, Oregon DAR Daughter

CHAMBERS, MATTHEW
Massachusetts, Oregon DAR Daughter

CHAMPLIN, CHARLES
DAR Daughter Belle Passi Chapter

CHANDLER, WILLIAM, PVT.
New Hampshire, Oregon DAR Daughter

CHAPIN, PHINEAS
Massachusetts, Oregon DAR Daughter

CHAPMAN, JAMES
Virginia, Oregon DAR Daughter

CHAPMAN, JOHN
Virginia, Oregon DAR Daughter

CHASE, BERRY, SGT.
New York, Oregon DAR Daughter

CHASE, CALEB
SAR Compatriots Keith Barnes, Wyatt Barnes

CHEESEBROUGH, PEREZ, PVT.
Connecticut, Oregon DAR Daughter

CHEESEMAN, RICHARD, CAPT.
New Jersey, Oregon DAR Daughter

CHENOWETH, THOMAS
Maryland, Oregon DAR Daughter

CHERRY, JOSHUA
　Virginia, Oregon DAR Daughter

CHILDS, DANIEL, JR.
　Massachusetts, Oregon DAR Daughter

CHILES, WILLIAM
　DAR Daughter Betty Mack

CHRISTIAN, PHILLIP, PVT., RANGER
　Pennsylvania, Oregon DAR Daughter

CHURCH, GILES, PVT.
　Massachusetts, SAR Compatriots Brian Perez, Brett Perez, Oregon DAR Daughter

CLAPP, SAMUEL
　Massachusetts, Oregon DAR Daughter

CLARK, BENJAMIN
　Connecticut,, Oregon DAR Daughter

CLARK, HEZEKIAH, PVT.
　Connecticut, Oregon DAR Daughter

CLARK, JAMES, PVT.
　Massachusetts, Oregon DAR Daughter

CLARK, JOHN
　Virginia, Oregon DAR Daughter

CLARK, JONAS
　Massachusetts, SAR Compatriot James Martin, Oregon DAR Daughter

CLARK, MATTHEW
　Massachusetts, Oregon DAR Daughter

CLARKE, ELISHA, PVT.
　Rhode Island, Oregon DAR Daughter

CLAYPOOLE, JOHN, SR.
　Virginia, Oregon DAR Daughter

CLEM, MICHAEL
　Virginia, Oregon DAR Daughter

CLENDENIN, JOHN
 Maryland, Oregon DAR Daughter

CLEVELAND, ISAAC
 Connecticut, Oregon DAR Daughter

CLEVELAND, JOSIAH
 SAR Compatriot John Raviolo

CLEVELAND, LARKIN, CAPT.
 North Carolina, Oregon DAR Daughter

CLEVELAND, WILLIAM, SR., PVT.
 Massachusetts, Oregon DAR Daughter

CLIFTON, NATHAN
 North Carolina, Oregon DAR Daughter

CLUGGAGE, GAVEN, CAPT.
 Pennsylvania, Oregon DAR Daughter

CLUTE, JOHN
 SAR Compatriots George Rogers, Michael Rogers

COCHRAN, JAMES
 Georgia,, Oregon DAR Daughter

COCKRUM, BENJAMIN
 Virginia, Oregon DAR Daughter

CODDINGTON, BENJAMIN
 New Jersey, Oregon DAR Daughter

COE, JOEL
 Connecticut, Oregon DAR Daughter

COFFEEN, HENRY
 New Hampshire, Oregon DAR Daughter

COFFIN, WILLIAM
 Massachusetts, Oregon DAR Daughter

COLBURN, BENJAMIN, PVT.
 New Hampshire Minuteman May 15, 1777 DAR Daughter Janice Gadway Gardner

COLBURN, ROBERT, SR.
New Hampshire DAR Daughter Janice Gadway Gardner.
Was one of 48 signers to the agreement to hold himself in readiness, as a Minute Man, at Hollis, NH 15th May 1777.

COLCLOUGH, WILLIAM
SAR Compatriots Tom Boardman, Edward Boardman

COLE, ABIEL
Massachusetts, Oregon DAR Daughter

COLE, JAMES, LT.
Virginia, Oregon DAR Daughter

COLE, JOSEPH
Virginia, Oregon DAR Daughter

COLEMAN, JACOB
SAR Compatriot Michael Mason

COLEMAN, JOHN
New Jersey, Oregon DAR Daughter

COLLIER, JOHN
South Carolina, Oregon DAR Daughter

COLTON, EBENEZER
Massachusetts, DAR Daughter Sue Proud

COMBS, JOHN, SR.
SAR Compatriot Wilbur Shakro

COMEGYS, ABRAHAM, SR.
Maryland, Oregon DAR Daughter

COMSTOCK, ABEL
Connecticut, Oregon DAR Daughter

COMSTOCK, MEDAD
Massachusetts, Oregon DAR Daughter

CONDIT, JABEZ
DAR Daughter Belle Passi Chapter

CONDIT, PHILIP
DAR Daughter Belle Passi Chapter

Cone, Joshua, Pvt.
Vermont, DAR Daughter Sue Glenn

Cone, William
Georgia, Oregon DAR Daughter

Conger, David
New Jersey, Oregon DAR Daughter

Cook, Eli
South Carolina, Oregon DAR Daughter

Cooke, Elisha
New Jersey, Oregon DAR Daughter

Coombs, John, Sr.
North Carolina, Oregon DAR Daughter

Coombs, Mason, Sr.
North Carolina, Oregon DAR Daughter

Coons, Jacob Jr.
Virginia, Oregon DAR Daughter

Cooper, Thomas, Pvt.
New York, Vermont, Oregon DAR Daughter

Copeland, Dennis
North Carolina, Oregon DAR Daughter

Corn, John Peter
North Carolina, Oregon DAR Daughter

Cornwell, William
SAR Compatriot William Cornwell

Correll, John
DAR Daughter Belle Passi Chapter

Corwin, Richard
New Jersey, Oregon DAR Daughter

Cotton, Samuel J.
Connecticut, Oregon DAR Daughter

COTTRELL, ASA
Massachusetts, Oregon DAR Daughter

COUCH, BENJAMIN, PVT.
Massachusetts, Oregon DAR Daughter

COULTER, ROBERT
DAR Daughter Belle Passi Chapter

COUNTRYMAN, CONRAD
New York, Oregon DAR Daughter

COVALT, ABRAHAM, CAPT.
Pennsylvania, Oregon DAR Daughter

COVELL, EZRA
Massachusetts, Oregon DAR Daughter

COVEY, WALTER
New York, Oregon DAR Daughter

COVINGTON, FRANCIS S.
Virginia, SAR Compatriot Albert Carder, Oregon DAR Daughter

COX, PHINEAS
SAR Compatriot Fred Isbell

COY, JOHN
Massachusetts, Oregon DAR Daughter

COYNER, CASPER
Pennsylvania, Oregon DAR Daughter

CRAIG, DAVID
North Carolina, Oregon DAR Daughter

CRAIG, MARY POLLY HAWKINS
Virginia, Oregon DAR Daughter

CRAPO, PETER, PVT.
Captain Levi Rounseville's Co. of Minutemen, SAR Compatriot Jerry Larsen
  April 19 -21, 1775 Private Peter Crapo in Captain Levi Rounseville's Company of minutemen which marched on the alarm of April 19, 1775 to Washington's camp at Cambridge. Service three days. Roll dated Roxbury Camp.

CRARY, NATHAN, PVT.
Connecticut, Vermont, Oregon DAR Daughter

CRAVEN, THOMAS
Pennsylvania, Oregon DAR Daughter

CRAWFORD, JAMES, ENS.
Pennsylvania, SAR Compatriot David Crawford,, Oregon DAR Daughter

CRAWFORD, JOEL
South Carolina, Oregon DAR Daughter

CRAW, REUBEN, PVT.
DAR Daughter Patti Waitman- Ingebretsen

CRESWELL, ROBERT, JR.
Pennsylvania, Oregon DAR Daughter

CRESWELL, WILLIAM
Maryland, Oregon DAR Daughter

CRIGLER, CHRISTOPHER
Virginia, Oregon DAR Daughter

CRONINGER, LEONARD , PVT.
Pennsylvania, Oregon DAR Daughter

CROSBY, HANNAH
South Carolina, Oregon DAR Daughter

CROSBY, STEPHEN
Connecticut, Oregon DAR Daughter

CROSBY, THOMAS, PVT.
South Carolina, Oregon DAR Daughter

CROWELL, HENRY
New York, Oregon DAR Daughter

CROW, JACOB, PVT.
Virginia, Oregon DAR Daughter

CRUM, RICHARD, PVT.
New York, Oregon DAR Daughter

CRUTCHLOW, JAMES, PVT.
Pennsylvania, Oregon DAR Daughter

CULBERTSON, ROBERT
Pennsylvania, Oregon DAR Daughter

CULVER, DAVID, PVT.
New York, Oregon DAR Daughter

CULVER, NATHANIEL
New York, Oregon DAR Daughter

CUMMINGS, NOBLE, PVT.
Massachusetts, DAR Daughter Sue Glenn

CURRIER, MOSES, PVT.
New Hampshire, Oregon DAR Daughter

CURRY, JAMES, CAPT.
Virginia, Oregon DAR Daughter

CUTLER, JOSEPH
Connecticut, Oregon DAR Daughter

D

DAGGETT, JOHN
Virginia, Oregon DAR Daughter

DALE, GEORGE
Virginia, Oregon DAR Daughter

DALTON, DAVID
Virginia, Oregon DAR Daughter

DALTON, JOHN
Pennsylvania, Oregon DAR Daughter

DALTON, SAMUEL, SR.
North Carolina, Oregon DAR Daughter

DANFORTH, DAVID
Massachusetts, Oregon DAR Daughter

DANFORTH, ENOCH
Massachusetts, Oregon DAR Daughter

DARON, ADAM, PVT.
Pennsylvania, Oregon DAR Daughter

DAVIDSON, JOHN
South Carolina, Oregon DAR Daughter

DAVIDSON, WILLIAM
Pennsylvania, Oregon DAR Daughter

DAVIS, CALEB
New Jersey, Oregon DAR Daughter

DAVIS, EDWARD
Virginia, Oregon DAR Daughter

DAVIS, ISSAC, SR.
Massachusetts, Oregon DAR Daughter

DAVIS, JAMES, PVT.
Massachusetts, Oregon DAR Daughter

DAVIS, JOHN
Massachusetts, Oregon DAR Daughter

DAVIS, PAUL
Massachusetts, Oregon DAR Daughter

DAVIS, SAMSON, SGT.
New York, Oregon DAR Daughter

DAVIS, WILLIAM, JR., PVT.
New Jersey, Oregon DAR Daughter

DAVIS, WILLIAM, SR., CAPT.
New Jersey, Oregon DAR Daughter

DAY, ABRAHAM
Massachusetts, Oregon DAR Daughter

DAY, EZERA
Massachusetts, Oregon DAR Daughter

DEAN, BENJAMIN, PVT.
Virginia, Oregon DAR Daughter

DEAN, ENOS, SGT.
Massachusetts, Oregon DAR Daughter

DEAN, JEDEDIAH
SAR Compatriot Thomas Eskridge

DEEDS, JOHN
Pennsylvania, Oregon DAR Daughter

DE HART, HENDRICK
New Jersey, Oregon DAR Daughter

DE LA ROCHE, FREDERICK FRANCK
France, Oregon DAR Daughter

DELANO, THOMAS, JR., SGTMAJ
Connecticut, New York, Oregon DAR Daughter

DE MERIT, JOHN II, MAJ.
New Hampshire, Oregon DAR Daughter

DE NORIEGA, JOSE VINCENTE GARCIA
South America, Oregon DAR Daughter

DENNEY, PATRICK
Virginia, Oregon DAR Daughter

DENNISON, DAVID
Vermont, Connecticut, Oregon DAR Daughter

DENT, JOHN
Virginia, Oregon DAR Daughter

DENTON, SOLOMON
DAR Daughter Belle Passi Chapter

DESCHLER, ADAM, OATH OF ALLEG.
Pennsylvania, Oregon DAR Daughter

DEUPREE (DUPREE), JOSEPH
Virginia, Oregon DAR Daughter

DEVIN, WILLIAM, JR.
SAR Compatriots David Devin, Gary Devin, Steven Devin, Michael Devin, DAR Daughter Belle Passi Chapter

DEWEESE, SAMUEL
Pennsylvania, Oregon DAR Daughter

DEWEY, STEPHEN
Massachusetts, Oregon DAR Daughter

DEWEY, WILLIAM, CPL.
Connecticut, New Hampshire, Oregon DAR Daughter

DEWING, JABEZ
Massachusetts, Oregon DAR Daughter

DEYO, PETER, PVT.
New York, Oregon DAR Daughter

DIAL, JOSEPH
SAR Compatriot Jan Dial

DICKS, JAMES
DAR Daughter Patti Waitman-Ingebretsen

DICKS, PETER
DAR Daughter Patti Waitman-Ingebretsen

DIEFENBAUGH, MICHAEL, LT.
Pennsylvania, Oregon DAR Daughter

DILLARD, WILLIAM, PVT.
Virginia, Oregon DAR Daughter

DILLEY, REVIDEL, PVT.
Connecticut, Oregon DAR Daughter

DIMMICK, ELIPHANT
Connecticut, Oregon DAR Daughter

DIMMICK, SOLOMON, LT.
Connecticut, Oregon DAR Daughter

DITTO, FRANCIS L., PVT.
2nd Pennsylvania Reg. SAR Compatriot Arlen Clark

DIX, ELIJAH
Massachusetts, Oregon DAR Daughter

DIXWELL, LOTHROP, PVT.
Connecticut, Oregon DAR Daughter

DOAK, DAVID, SR.
Virginia, Oregon DAR Daughter

DODSON, GEORGE
SAR Compatriot Shawn O'Neil

DOLSON, JOHN, SGT.
Pennsylvania, Oregon DAR Daughter

DONALDSON, ISAAC, PVT.
Pennsylvania, Oregon DAR Daughter

DORRANCE, SAMUEL, PVT.
Rhode Island, Oregon DAR Daughter

DORSEY, DANIEL, CAPT.
Maryland, Oregon DAR Daughter

DOTY, PHILLIP, SGT.
New York, Oregon DAR Daughter

DOTY, WILLIAM, NONCOM.
Connecticut, Oregon DAR Daughter

DOUSE, JOSEPH, SGT.
Massachusetts, Oregon DAR Daughter

DOWLER, EDWARD
Pennsylvania, Oregon DAR Daughter

DOWNEY, DARB, CAPT.
Virginia, Oregon DAR Daughter

DOYLE, BARNABAS, PVT.
Pennsylvania, Oregon DAR Daughter

DRAKE, GEORGE
New Jersey, Oregon DAR Daughter

DRAKE, THOMAS
  DAR Daughter Belle Passi Chapter

DRAPER, JOHN
  Massachusetts, Oregon DAR Daughter

DUDLEY, ASA, PVT.
  Connecticut, Oregon DAR Daughter

DUDLEY, SAMUEL, STAFF OFFICER
  New Hampshire, Oregon DAR Daughter

DUER, JOHN
  SAR Compatriot Richard Duer

DUMONT, PETER, SGT.
  Col. Wynkoop Reg., New York SAR Compatriot Arlen Clark

DUNBAR, THOMAS
  Massachusetts, Oregon DAR Daughter

DUNCAN, ELIZABETH ALEXANDER
  Virginia, Oregon DAR Daughter

DUNCAN, MOSES
  South Carolina, Oregon SAR Compatriot

DUNCAN, WILLIAM, SR.
  Pennsylvania, Oregon DAR Daughter

DUNHAM, JOHN, PVT.
  Massachusetts, Oregon DAR Daughter

DUNLAP, SAMUEL, PVT.
  Pennsylvania, Oregon DAR Daughter

DUNNINGTON, WILLIAM, JR.
  Maryland, Oregon DAR Daughter

DUNNINGTON, WILLIAM, SR.
  Maryland, Oregon DAR Daughter

DURFEE, GIDEON, PVT.
  Rhode Island, Oregon DAR Daughter

DURKEE, BENJAMIN
Connecticut, Oregon DAR Daughter

DUTCHER, CORNELIUS
Massachusetts, Oregon DAR Daughter

DYE, ANDREW
Pennsylvania, Oregon DAR Daughter

DYER, HENRY, JR.
SAR Compatriots Charles Martin, Joseph Martin

DYSART, JOHN, SGT.
North Carolina, Oregon DAR Daughter

E

EAGER, WILLIAM
New York, Oregon DAR Daughter

EATON, WILLIAM
Virginia, Oregon DAR Daughter

EBAUGH, JOHN
Pennsylvania, SAR Compatriots Geoffrey Knox, Michael Nakahara, Kenneth Nakahara, Oregon DAR Daughter

ECK, THEODORUS, PVT.
Pennsylvania, Oregon DAR Daughter

EDDY, ABEL
New Hampshire, Oregon DAR Daughter

EDDY, ZACHARIAH
Massachusetts, Oregon DAR Daughter

EDGINGTON, JOSEPH
Pennsylvania, Oregon DAR Daughter

EDWARDS, DAVID
North Carolina, Oregon DAR Daughter

EDWARDS, JOHN, SR.
North Carolina, Oregon DAR Daughter

ELDER, ROBERT
Pennsylvania, Oregon DAR Daughter

ELDREGE (ELDRIDGE), PHINEAS
Pennsylvania, Oregon DAR Daughter

ELKINS, ROBERT
Virginia, Oregon DAR Daughter

ELSTON, DAVID, SGT.
New Jersey, Oregon DAR Daughter

EMERSON, JONATHAN
New Hampshire, Oregon DAR Daughter

EMERY, AMBROSE, PVT.
Pennsylvania, Oregon DAR Daughter

ENGLE. PHILLIP
Virginia, Oregon DAR Daughter

ERWIN, ARTHUR, COL.
Pennsylvania, SAR Compatriots Phillip Erwin, Riley Erwin, Jackson Erwin

Col. Arthur Erwin, born in 1726, a Scotch-Irish immigrant of considerable means, came from County Antrim, Ireland, and settled at Erwinna, Bucks County, Pennsylvania, in 1768.

The family, consisting of his wife, Mary Scott Erwin, and seven children, sailed from Newry on a ship called the Newry Assistance about May 1st, and landed at Philadelphia, Pa., August 18,1768. The wife and an infant born at sea, had died and been buried at sea about the tenth of July.

In 1776 - 77 Arthur Erwin was Colonel respectively of the Fourth and Second Battalions of the Bucks County Militia, in which several letters and orders, which are still in existence, were addressed to him by General Washington, just previous to the Battle of Trenton, the Christmas Eve before the battle. "Col. Erwin carried many of our soldiers across the river in his own boats, from his estate on the banks of the Delaware."

He was shot and killed at Tioga Point, supposedly by a squatter,

June 9, 1791.

Col. Erwin possessed large tracts of land also in Luzerne County, Pennsylvania, and Steuben County, New York.

Before his arrival in 1768, Col. Arthur and his brother, William Erwin, had not only visited this country, but had purchased large tracts of land in Tinicum township, Bucks County, Pennsylvania.

ERWIN, FRANCIS
Virginia, Oregon DAR Daughter

ESKRIDGE, BURDETT
South Carolina, Oregon DAR Daughter

ESSELSTYNE, CONRADT
New York, Oregon DAR Daughter

ESTABROOK, EBENEZER
Massachusetts, Oregon DAR Daughter

EUBANK, JOHN
Virginia, Oregon DAR Daughter

EVANS, JOHN, COL.
Virginia, Oregon DAR Daughter

EVERETT, EBENEZER, SR.
Connecticut, Oregon DAR Daughter

EWER, JOHN
Pennsylvania, Oregon DAR Daughter

EWING, WILLIAM, PVT.
Pennsylvania, Oregon DAR Daughter

EZELL, JOHN
Virginia, Oregon DAR Daughter

F

FAIRBANKS, JOHN, LT.
Massachusetts, Oregon DAR Daughter

FAIRFIELD, WILLIAM
Connecticut, Oregon DAR Daughter

FANNIN, LAUGHLIN, OFFICER
Virginia, Oregon DAR Daughter

FARLEY, DANIEL, PVT.
Virginia, Oregon DAR Daughter

FARMER, JAMES
Virginia, Oregon DAR Daughter

FARMUM, LEVI
Connecticut, Oregon DAR Daughter

FARR, THOMAS
Massachusetts, Oregon DAR Daughter

FARRINGTON, FREDERICK, PVT.
Massachusetts, Oregon DAR Daughter

FAUCETT, WILLIAM
DAR Daughter Patti Waitman-Ingebretsen

FAUST, ADAM
Pennsylvania, Oregon DAR Daughter

FEARING, ABEL, PVT.
Massachusetts, Oregon DAR Daughter

FEARING, JAMES, PVT.
Massachusetts, Oregon DAR Daughter

FELTON, BENJAMIN, LT. ADJ.
Massachusetts, Oregon DAR Daughter

FENTON, SAMUEL, CAPT.
DAR Daughter Patti Waitman-Ingebretsen

FERGUSON, DAVID
SAR Compatriot Charles Thompson

FERGUSON, JOHN
Massachusetts, Oregon DAR Daughter

FIELD, JOHN VAN WYCK
   New York, Oregon DAR Daughter

FINLEY, JAMES
   Pennsylvania, Oregon DAR Daughter

FISHER, JACOB
   DAR Daughter Belle Passi Chapter

FISK, WILLIAM
   Connecticut, Oregon DAR Daughter

FITCH, TIMOTHY
   Connecticut, Oregon DAR Daughter

FLAGG, PETER, PVT.
   New York, Oregon DAR Daughter

FLEMING, ELIJAH
   South Carolina, Oregon DAR Daughter

FLEMING, ROBERT, SR.
   South Carolina, Oregon DAR Daughter

FLETCHER, BENJAMIN
   Connecticut, Oregon DAR Daughter

FLINT, WILLIAM
   Massachusetts, Oregon DAR Daughter

FLOOD, DANIEL, PVT.
   New Hampshire, Oregon DAR Daughter

FLORA, JOSEPH J., SR.
   Patriot, Lancaster Co., Pennsylvania SAR Compatriot Arlen Clark

FOGELSANGER, JACOB
   Pennsylvania, Oregon DAR Daughter

FOLSOM, DANIEL
   New Hampshire, Oregon DAR Daughter

FOOTE, HENRY
   SAR Compatriots Tom Boardman, Edward Boardman

FORD, JACOB, SR.
Committee to form Union of Colonies, Morris Co. New Jersey
SAR Compatriot Johnny Alexander

FORE, PETER
North Carolina, Oregon DAR Daughter

FORQUERAN, JOHN
Virginia, Oregon DAR Daughter

FORQUERAN, PETER, SR.
Virginia, Oregon DAR Daughter

FORTSON, THOMAS
Virginia, Oregon DAR Daughter

FOSTER, EZEKIEL
Oregon DAR Daughter

FOSTER, HEZEKIAH, PVT.
New Hampshire, Oregon DAR Daughter

FOSTER, RICHARD
Massachusetts, Oregon DAR Daughter

FOSTER, RICHARD, SR.
Massachusetts, Oregon DAR Daughter

FOWLER, GODFREY
North Carolina, Oregon DAR Daughter

FOWLER, JOSHUA, CPL.
South Carolina, Oregon DAR Daughter

FRANCISCO, LUDWICK
Virginia, Oregon DAR Daughter

FRENCH, SEBA, CPL.
Massachusetts, Oregon DAR Daughter

FRINK, ISAAC
Connecticut, SAR Compatriot Thomas Akers, Oregon DAR Daughter

Frink, Ruth Pinckney
South Carolina, Oregon DAR Daughter

Frisbie, Philemon
Connecticut, Oregon DAR Daughter

Frost, Samuel
Massachusetts, Oregon DAR Daughter

Fruge, Pierre Antoine
Oregon DAR Daughter

Frutchey, Frederick
Pennsylvania, Oregon DAR Daughter

Fuller, Abraham
Connecticut, Oregon DAR Daughter

Fullerton, Alexander
Pennsylvania, Oregon DAR Daughter

Fuson, William
Virginia, Oregon DAR Daughter

Futrell, Thomas
North Carolina, Oregon DAR Daughter

G

Gaines, Ambrose
Virginia, Oregon DAR Daughter

Gaines, Thomas, Cpl.
Virginia, Oregon DAR Daughter

Gambil, Martin
North Carolina, Oregon DAR Daughter

Gano, James
New Jersey, Oregon DAR Daughter

Gard, Daniel
New Jersey, Oregon DAR Daughter

GARDNER, JOHN
   Pennsylvania, Oregon DAR Daughter

GARDNER, JOSEPH
   New Jersey, Oregon DAR Daughter

GARDNER, MARTIN
   Pennsylvania, Oregon DAR Daughter

GARDNER, WILLIAM
   New Jersey, Oregon DAR Daughter

GARNETT, ANTHONY, CPL.
   Virginia, Oregon DAR Daughter

GARNETT, REUBEN
   Virginia, Oregon DAR Daughter

GARRETT, AMBROSE
   Virginia, Oregon DAR Daughter

GARRETT, FRANCIS, JR., PVT.
   Connecticut, Oregon DAR Daughter

GARRISON, JAMES
   North Carolina, Oregon DAR Daughter

GARVIN, THOMAS, SGT.
   Pennsylvania, Oregon DAR Daughter

GARVIN, THOMAS, PVT.
   Pennsylvania, Oregon DAR Daughter

GASS, DAVID, SR.
   Virginia, Oregon DAR Daughter

GATES, JONATHAN, PVT.
   Massachusetts, Oregon DAR Daughter

GATES, SILAS, PVT.
   Connecticut, Oregon DAR Daughter

GAULT, MATTHEW
   Pennsylvania, Oregon DAR Daughter

GAYLORD, AARON, LT.
Connecticut, Oregon DAR Daughter

GENTRY, BENEJAH
Virginia, Oregon DAR Daughter

GENUNG, THOMAS
New Jersey, Oregon DAR Daughter

GERARD, JOHN
Oregon DAR Daughter

GIBBS, HEZEKIAH
Massachusetts, Oregon DAR Daughter

GIFFIN, EDWARD
Vermont, Oregon DAR Daughter

GIFFIN, JOHN
Massachusetts, Oregon DAR Daughter

GIFFIN, SIMON
Connecticut, Oregon DAR Daughter

GIFT, JOHAN A., PVT.
5th Class, Rangers 1st Bat., Cumberland Co., Pennsylvania SAR Compatriot Arlen Clark

GILBERT, GARDNER
Connecticut, Oregon DAR Daughter

GILBERT, JOSEPH, SGT.
Connecticut, Oregon DAR Daughter

GILHAM, PETER
Virginia, Oregon DAR Daughter

GILLAM, JONATHAN, PVT.
Pennsylvania, Oregon DAR Daughter

GILLESPIE, DANIEL, CAPT.
North Carolina, Oregon DAR Daughter

GILLETTE, JOSEPH
Connecticut, Oregon DAR Daughter

GILLIAM, HINCHEA
Virginia, Oregon DAR Daughter

GILLIAM, JAMES
Virginia, Oregon DAR Daughter

GILLIHAN, WILLIAM, PVT.
Virginia, Oregon DAR Daughter

GILSTRAP, PETER
North Carolina, Oregon DAR Daughter

GISH, CHRISTIAN, SR.
Pennsylvania, Oregon DAR Daughter

GISH, GEORGE
Pennsylvania, Oregon DAR Daughter

GISH, JOHN G.
Pennsylvania, Oregon DAR Daughter

GLANTZ, JOHANNES, PVT.
Pennsylvania, Oregon DAR Daughter

GLASS, JOHANN MATHIAS
Pennsylvania, Oregon DAR Daughter

GLAZIER, JOHN, PVT.
South Carolina, Oregon DAR Daughter

GLIDDEN, BENJAMIN
Oregon DAR Daughter

GOBLE, STEPHEN
New Jersey, Oregon DAR Daughter

GOFF, JOHN, SR.
New Hampshire, Oregon DAR Daughter

GOIN, THOMAS
Virginia, DAR Daughter Belle Passi Chapter

GOLDSMITH, JOHN, SR.
Virginia, Oregon DAR Daughter

GOODE, SAMUEL
Pennsylvania, Oregon DAR Daughter

GOODRICH, ELNATHAN
Connecticut, Oregon DAR Daughter

GOODRICH, JAMES
Massachusetts, Oregon DAR Daughter

GOODRICH, THOMAS, PVT.
Massachusetts, Oregon DAR Daughter

GOODRICH, WAITSTILL
Connecticut, DAR Daughter Belle Passi Chapter

GOODSON, WILLIAM, ENS.
Virginia, Oregon DAR Daughter

GORDON, JESSE
SAR Compatriots Brayden Arsenault, Dean Boring

GORMLEY, HUGH
DAR Daughter Belle Passi Chapter

GOSS, ELIZABETH X
Pennsylvania, Oregon DAR Daughter

GOTT, STORY
New York, Oregon DAR Daughter

GOULD, SOLOMON
Massachusetts, Oregon DAR Daughter

GOURLEY, HUGH
South Carolina, Oregon DAR Daughter

GRAHAM, PETER, PVT.
North Carolina, Oregon DAR Daughter

GRAMMER, JOSEPH, PVT.
French, Legion of Lauzun, under Major John L. Polerescky, 1780-1782 SAR Compatriot Christopher Matheny
    Joseph Grammer was born in 1762 in Haguenau, Alsace, France. At age 18, as the youngest son in the family whose father died in 1763, Joseph volunteered in the Legions of Lauzun with

the stated purpose of going to America to assist the Americans in the Revolutionary struggle for Liberty. His journey from Brest France to Rhode Island during the summer of 1780 included a severe naval engagement with British forces, Joseph wrote: "the firing commenced middle of the afternoon and continued until night, the enemy were vanquished as they were not to be found the next morning."
After arrival he was marched up to Hartford Connecticut where he continued that winter, a winter so cold that his Major Polerescky wrote he thought it much like Siberia.

Then during the summer of 1781, he was marched to white plains New York where he assisted the main American army in what Joseph described as "the severe Battle at the white plains".

Thereafter he was marched to Little York and was in the celebrated siege from the commencement until Lord Cornwallis "was taken."

The Legion stayed the winter in Hampton, Virginia then marched in the spring to Charlotte Virginia. Then on the 8th of June, with the Legion due to start the journey back to France on the 10th, Joseph stated he received a "verbal discharge". Joseph, along with many of his French compatriots, wanted to stay in the new America they helped create.

Joseph stayed in Charlotte where, according to tax records at the time, he worked on local farms.

In June of 1787 he married Elizabeth Pryor and shortly thereafter they moved from Charlotte to the Rich Patch area in Botetourt County Virginia to try his hand at farming. Life was hard for Joseph and the tax and court records show that he moved from Botetourt to Russell then Lee Counties in Virginia and finally settled in Roane County Tennessee. In 1833 he applied for a pension as a veteran of the Revolutionary War. Alas, his pension application was rejected for the stated cause that there was no provision in the law for a French soldier. Joseph died in Tennessee about 1852, the father of 12 children. Three of his sons joined the US Army; two in the war of 1812, one of whom died in that war.

GRANT, BENJAMIN, PVT.
Rhode Island, Oregon DAR Daughter

GRANT, WILLIAM, SR.
North Carolina, Virginia, Oregon DAR Daughter

GRAVES, ANN
Virginia, Oregon DAR Daughter

GRAVES, DAVID
North Carolina, Oregon DAR Daughter

GRAVES, JOHN
Virginia, Oregon DAR Daughter

GREELY, SHUBAL
New Hampshire, Pennsylvania, Oregon DAR Daughter

GREENLEE, WILLIAM, PVT.
Pennsylvania, SAR Compatriot Elton Clark, Oregon DAR Daughter

GREENWOOD, BARTLEE
Virginia, Oregon DAR Daughter

GREGG, ISRAEL, PVT.
Pennsylvania, Oregon DAR Daughter

GREGG, ROBERT
DAR Daughter Belle Passi Chapter

GREGORY, URIAH
DAR Daughter Belle Passi Chapter

GRIER, HENRY, LT.
Proctors Continental Artillery Reg., 5th Continental Artillery Reg. 1777-1789 SAR Compatriot Grier Ingebretsen
Commander Thomas Proctor Battles involved in: Trenton 1776, Assunpink Creek 1777, Princeton 1777, Bound Creek 1777, Brandywine 1777, Germantown 1777, Monmouth 1778, Sullivan Expedition 1779, Bulls Ferry 1780, Green Spring 1781, Yorktown 1781, Southern Theater 1781-1782.

GRIER, JOHN
South Carolina, Oregon DAR Daughter

GRIER, THOMAS
South Carolina, Oregon DAR Daughter

GRIFFIN, SHERROD, SGT.
Virginia, Oregon DAR Daughter

GRISWOLD, JOHN, PVT.
Connecticut, Oregon DAR Daughter

GUILLION, JEREMIAH, PVT.
Pennsylvania, Oregon DAR Daughter

GUNNISON, SAMUEL, SR., CAPT.
New Hampshire, Oregon DAR Daughter

GUTHREY, HENRY
Virginia, Oregon DAR Daughter

H

HADLEY, SIMON
North Carolina, Oregon DAR Daughter

HAGGARD, NATHANIEL
Virginia, Oregon DAR Daughter

HALE, ISAAC
Connecticut, Oregon DAR Daughter

HALE, REUBEN
Connecticut, Oregon DAR Daughter

HALFERTY, EDWARD, PVT.
Pennsylvania, Oregon DAR Daughter

HALL, CALEB
Virginia, Oregon DAR Daughter

HALL, DAVID
North Carolina, Oregon DAR Daughter

HALL, EDWARD, PVT.
North Carolina, Oregon DAR Daughter

HALL, GEORGE ABBOTT
South Carolina, Oregon DAR Daughter

HALL, JAMES
DAR Daughter Patti Waitman-Ingebretsen

HALL, LAWRENCE RUBIN
Maryland, Oregon DAR Daughter

HALL, LEONARD
Virginia, Oregon DAR Daughter

HALLEY, FRANCIS
SAR Compatriot Larry Heckethorne

HALLEY, JAMES, SR.
Virginia, Oregon DAR Daughter

HALSEY, JOHN, PVT.
New Jersey, Oregon DAR Daughter

HALSEY, SYLVANUS
SAR Compatriot Ernest Cowan

HAMAR, JAMES, PVT.
New Jersey, Oregon DAR Daughter

HAMILTON, SILAS
Connecticut, Oregon DAR Daughter

HANDY, SAMUEL
Maryland, Oregon DAR Daughter

HANEY, ROBERT
SAR Compatriot John Haney

HANLIN, PATRICK
SAR Compatriot Paul O'Hanlon

HAPGOOD, ASA, JR., PVT.
Massachusetts, Oregon DAR Daughter

HARBAUGH, YOST, CAPT.
Pennsylvania, Oregon DAR Daughter

HARBOUR, JOEL, PVT.
Virginia, Oregon DAR Daughter

HARDAWAY, JOHN, LT.
Virginia, Oregon DAR Daughter

HARDAWAY, THOMAS
  Virginia, Oregon DAR Daughter

HARDING, HENRY, SR.
  Virginia, Oregon DAR Daughter

HARDING, STEPHEN
  SAR Compatriots Kevin Harding, Ian Harding

HARDING, WILMOTH GEORGE
  Virginia, Oregon DAR Daughter

HARDY, EPHRAIM
  DAR Daughter Belle Passi Chapter

HARKER, DANIEL
  New Jersey, Oregon DAR Daughter

HARKER, JOSEPH
  SAR Compatriots John Bogardus, Bradley Bogardus, Brian Bogardus

HARLOW, ZACHEUS
  Massachusetts, Oregon DAR Daughter

HARMON, JOHN
  Connecticut, Oregon DAR Daughter

HARMON, THOMAS
  Virginia, Oregon DAR Daughter

HARPER, RICHARD, PVT.
  North Carolina, Oregon DAR Daughter

HARRAVE, JOHN, SR., PVT.
  South Carolina, Oregon DAR Daughter

HARRINGTON, HENRY
  Rhode Island, Oregon DAR Daughter

HARRINGTON, SAMPSON
  Oregon DAR Daughter

HARRINGTON, THOMAS
  Rhode Island, Oregon DAR Daughter

HARRIS, HENRY
Virginia, Oregon DAR Daughter

HARRIS, NICHOLAS
New Jersey, Oregon DAR Daughter

HARRISON, JAMES MASON
Virginia, Oregon DAR Daughter

HARSHMAN, PETER
Virginia, Oregon DAR Daughter

HART, TIMOTHY, SGT.
Connecticut, Oregon DAR Daughter

HARVEY, THOMAS, PVT.
Virginia, Oregon DAR Daughter

HARVEY, WILLIAM, PVT.
Connecticut, Oregon DAR Daughter

HARVEY, ZEPHONIAH
SAR Compatriot William Phillips

HASKELL, JOSIAH, PVT.
Massachusetts, Oregon DAR Daughter

HASKELL, WILLIAM
Massachusetts, Oregon DAR Daughter

HASKINS, EBENEZER, SGT.
Massachusetts, Oregon DAR Daughter

HASSAN, HUGH
Pennsylvania, Oregon DAR Daughter

HATCH, JETHRO, MAJ.
Connecticut, Oregon DAR Daughter

HATCH, JOSEPH
DAR Daughter Belle Passi Chapter

HAWES, ICHABOD, PVT.
Massachusetts, Oregon DAR Daughter

HAWKINS, AMAZIAH
   Connecticut, Oregon DAR Daughter

HAWKINS, URIAH
   Rhode Island, Oregon DAR Daughter

HAWKS, ABJAH
   Massachusetts, Oregon DAR Daughter

HAYCRAFT, SAMUEL
   Virginia, Oregon DAR Daughter

HAYNES, JONATHON
   Massachusetts, Oregon DAR Daughter

HAYNES, THOMAS
   Massachusetts, Maryland, Oregon DAR Daughter

HAYNIE, WILLIAM, 2ND LT.
   Virginia, Oregon DAR Daughter

HEAD, BENJAMIN, CAPT.
   Virginia, Oregon DAR Daughter

HEAD, JAMES, ENS.
   Virginia, Oregon DAR Daughter

HEALD, BENJAMIN, PVT.
   Massachusetts, Oregon DAR Daughter

HEALD, EPHRAIM
   Massachusetts, Oregon DAR Daughter

HEARD, THOMAS
   Virginia, Oregon DAR Daughter

HEATH, JOSEPH JR.
   New York, Oregon DAR Daughter

HEATH, JOSHUA
   New Hampshire, Oregon DAR Daughter

HELFFERICH, JOHN, JR., PVT.
   Pennsylvania, Oregon DAR Daughter

HENDERSON, PLEASANT, MAJ.
North Carolina, Oregon DAR Daughter

HENDREN/HENDRON, JOHN
North Carolina, Oregon DAR Daughter

HENNING, CHRISTOPHEL
DAR Daughter Belle Passi Chapter

HERRICK, AMOS
Vermont, Oregon DAR Daughter

HERRICK, HENRY, SGT.
Massachusetts, Oregon DAR Daughter

HESLEY, LENARD, PVT.
Pennsylvania, Oregon DAR Daughter

HESTER, ABRAHAM
North Carolina, Oregon DAR Daughter

HEWITT, NICHOLAS
Massachusetts, Oregon DAR Daughter

HICHBORN, ROBERT, LT.
Massachusetts, Oregon DAR Daughter

HIGLEY, JOEL, 2ND LT.
Inspector of Provisions, Connecticut 1778- ? SAR Compatriot William Guiel, Oregon DAR Daughter

Inspector of Provisions, Connecticut Birth: 1 August 1739 at Simsbury, Hartford Co., CT. Resided at Simsbury, Hartford Co., CT. Death: March 1, 1794 at Gallia Co., OH. The military instinct developed in Joel Higley is in line with his father, his grandfather, and his great-grandfather.

He was commissioned to the rank of lieutenant in the North Train Band in 1778, and served in this rank during the remaining part of the War of the Revolution. He appears to have followed agricultural pursuits during his entire life, living peacefully and quietly in the society of his kindred and neighbors. He was clever and genial, given to rough humor and exceedingly fond of practical jokes.

HIGLEY, SETH
SAR Compatriot Robert Bogardus

HILL, JOHN
New Hampshire, Oregon DAR Daughter

HILL, THOMAS
DAR Daughter Belle Passi Chapter

HILLER, MARTIN, PVT.
Pennsylvania, Oregon DAR Daughter

HILLEY, THOMAS
Virginia, Oregon DAR Daughter

HILLIARD, DANIEL, SMN
Connecticut & Massachusetts, Oregon DAR Daughter

HILTZ, GODFREY/GOTFRIED
DAR Daughter Belle Passi Chapter

HINCH, SAMUEL
Virginia, Oregon DAR Daughter

HINKLE, JOHN JUSTUS
Virginia, Oregon DAR Daughter

HISEY, JOHN
DAR Daughter Belle Passi Chapter

HITCHCOCK, PHINEAS, SR., PVT.
Massachusetts, Oregon DAR Daughter

HITT, PETER
Virginia, Oregon DAR Daughter

HIXON/HICKSON, JOHN
New Jersey, Oregon DAR Daughter

HOBLIT, JOHANNES MICHAEL, PVT.
Pennsylvania, Oregon DAR Daughter

HOCKENBERRY, CASPER
Pennsylvania, Oregon DAR Daughter

HOCKENBERRY, PETER
Pennsylvania, Oregon DAR Daughter

HODGE, CHARLES
Massachusetts, Oregon DAR Daughter

HOGG, JAMES
North Carolina, Oregon DAR Daughter

HOLBROOK, SILAS, SURG MATE
Massachusetts, Oregon DAR Daughter

HOLLAND, THOMAS
Virginia, Oregon DAR Daughter

HOLLEMAN, JESSE
Virginia, Oregon DAR Daughter

HOLLIS, ELIJAH
Massachusetts, Oregon DAR Daughter

HOLLOWAY, ELKANAH
New Jersey, Oregon DAR Daughter

HOLLOWAY, THOMAS
North Carolina, Oregon DAR Daughter

HOLMAN, ELISHA, SGT.
Massachusetts, Oregon DAR Daughter

HOLMES, JAMES
Massachusetts, Oregon DAR Daughter

HOLMES, LEMUEL, CAPT.
Massachusetts, New Hampshire, Oregon DAR Daughter

HOOPER, ABSALOM
South Carolina, Georgia, Oregon DAR Daughter

HOOPES, EZRA
Pennsylvania, Oregon DAR Daughter

HOOVER, HENRY
New Jersey, Oregon DAR Daughter

HORTON, NATHANIEL, PVT.
New Jersey, Oregon DAR Daughter

HOTCHKISS, DANIEL, PVT.
Connecticut, Oregon DAR Daughter

HOTCHKISS, MARK
Connecticut, Oregon DAR Daughter

HOTTENSTEIN, JACOB
SAR Compatriot John Hortenstine

HOUSTON, JAMES
Pennsylvania, Oregon DAR Daughter

HOUTZ, JACOB
DAR Daughter Belle Passi Chapter

HOVEY, SAMUEL
Massachusetts, Oregon DAR Daughter

HOWARD, PETER
Virginia, Oregon DAR Daughter

HOWES, JEREMIAH
Massachusetts, Oregon DAR Daughter

HOWLAND, CALEB
DAR Daughter Belle Passi Chapter

HOWLAND, JON, JR.
Rhode Island, Oregon DAR Daughter

HOYT, JONATHAN
Connecticut, Oregon DAR Daughter

HOYT, THOMAS, PVT.
New Hampshire, Oregon DAR Daughter

HUTCHINSON, JAMES, PVT.
New Jersey, Oregon DAR Daughter

HUDSON, DAVID
Virginia, Oregon DAR Daughter

HUDSON, WILLIAM
Virginia, Oregon DAR Daughter

HUGHES, JONATHAN
SAR Compatriot Nathan Rupert

HUGHEY, JAMES, SGT.
South Carolina, Oregon DAR Daughter

HUME, GEORGE
Virginia, Oregon DAR Daughter

HUMPHREY, ELISHA
Virginia, Oregon DAR Daughter

HUNTER, DAVID
Massachusetts, Oregon DAR Daughter

HUNTER, HENRY, PVT.
North Carolina, Oregon DAR Daughter

HURST, HENRY
DAR Daughter Belle Passi Chapter

HUSH, VALENTINE
DAR Daughter Belle Passi Chapter

HUTCHINSON, CORNELIUS
Pennsylvania, Oregon DAR Daughter

I

INGALLS, ISRAEL, SGT.
New Hampshire, Oregon DAR Daughter

INGHAM, ALEXANDER, PVT.
Connecticut, Oregon DAR Daughter

INGRAHAM , DUNCAN
Massachusetts, Oregon DAR Daughter

IRWIN, JOHN
South Carolina, Oregon DAR Daughter

IVES, NATHANIEL, JR., PVT.
Vermont, Oregon DAR Daughter

IVES, NATHANIEL, SR.
Connecticut, Oregon DAR Daughter

J

JAMES, ARRON
Pennsylvania, Oregon DAR Daughter

JENKINS., JOHN, JR.
Pennsylvania, Oregon DAR Daughter

JENKINS, JOHN, SR.
Pennsylvania, Oregon DAR Daughter

JEWETT, MOSES, SR., CAPT.
Massachusetts, Oregon DAR Daughter

JOHNSON, GRIFFITH, CAPT.
Maryland, Oregon DAR Daughter

JOHNSON, MOSES
New Hampshire, Oregon DAR Daughter

JOHNSON, ROBERT
North Carolina, Oregon DAR Daughter

JOHNSTON, ZACHARIAH, CAPT.
Virginia, Oregon DAR Daughter

JONES, ADAM CRANE, SR., CAPT.
South Carolina, Oregon DAR Daughter

JONES, JACOB
Pennsylvania, Oregon DAR Daughter

JONES, JOHN
SAR Compatriot Shawn O'Neil

JONES, RUSSELL
North Carolina, Oregon DAR Daughter

JONES, THOMAS, MAJ.
Maryland, Oregon DAR Daughter

JORDAN, WILLIAM
SAR Compatriot Solon Webb

JOSEPH, DANIEL
Virginia, Oregon DAR Daughter

JOSLIN, HEZEKIAH
SAR Compatriot Jeffrey Smith

JOYNER, THOMAS
North Carolina, Oregon DAR Daughter

JUNKIN, JOSEPH
Pennsylvania, Oregon DAR Daughter

JUSTICE, RALPH
Furnished Supplies Accomac Co., Virginia SAR Compatriots Eugene Melvin, Michael Melvin, Christopher Williams

K

KEES, PHILLIP
Pennsylvania, Oregon DAR Daughter

KELLER, CHRISTOPHER
SAR Compatriots Bruce Keller, Harpel Keller

KELLOG, ELIJAH
SAR Compatriot David Shoemaker

KELLOGG, JASON
Massachusetts, Oregon DAR Daughter

KELLY, HENRY
North Carolina, Oregon DAR Daughter

KEMMERER, JACOB
DAR Daughter Belle Passi Chapter

KEMPER, TILLMAN, PVT.
Virginia, Oregon DAR Daughter

KENT, ABSALOM, ENS.
Pennsylvania, Oregon DAR Daughter

KENT, CEPHAS, JR.
Vermont, Oregon DAR Daughter

KENT, THOMAS
Maryland, Oregon DAR Daughter

KETCHAM, JOSHUA
New York, Oregon DAR Daughter

KIBBE, MOSES
DAR Daughter Belle Passi Chapter

KILGORE, PATRICK
Pennsylvania, Oregon DAR Daughter

KIMBALL, AARON
Massachusetts, Oregon DAR Daughter

KIMBALL, ABRAHAM
SAR Compatriots Brandon Smith, Cameron Smith, Roger Swim

KIMMEL, NICHOLAS
DAR Daughter Belle Passi Chapter

KING, AMOS
Massachusetts, Oregon DAR Daughter

KING, HERMAN
New York, Oregon DAR Daughter

KING, JOHN
Virginia, Oregon DAR Daughter

KIZER, CHARLES
Virginia, Oregon DAR Daughter

KLINE, LORENTZ, PVT.
Pennsylvania, Oregon DAR Daughter

KLOCK, GEORGE
New York, Oregon DAR Daughter

Klock, George G.
New York, Oregon DAR Daughter

Klotz, Johann Leonhard
Pennsylvania, Oregon DAR Daughter

Knight, Samuel
Massachusetts, Oregon DAR Daughter

Knox, John, Lt.
South Carolina, Oregon DAR Daughter

Koiner, George
Pennsylvania, Oregon DAR Daughter

Kroesen, Isaac, Pvt.
Virginia, Oregon DAR Daughter

Krom, John
DAR Daughter Belle Passi Chapter

L

Lackland, Aaron
Maryland, Oregon DAR Daughter

Ladd, John, Pvt.
DAR Daughter Patti Waitman-Ingebretsen

Lake, Asa
Vermont, Oregon DAR Daughter

Lake, Gershom
Vermont, Oregon DAR Daughter

Lampkin, James
Virginia, Oregon DAR Daughter

Lance, John
Pennsylvania, Oregon DAR Daughter

Land, Moses
Virginia, Oregon DAR Daughter

LANDIS, JACOB, PVT.
5th Class, Lancaster Co., Pennsylvania Militia SAR Compatriot Arlen Clark

LANE, EDWARD
Pennsylvania, Oregon DAR Daughter

LANE, JAMES
Virginia, Oregon DAR Daughter

LANE, SAMUEL, PVT.
Pennsylvania, Oregon DAR Daughter

LANE, TIDENCE, JR, PVT.
North Carolina, Oregon DAR Daughter

LANGWORTHY, JAMES, PVT.
Vermont, Oregon DAR Daughter

LANIER, BURWELL
North Carolina, Oregon DAR Daughter

LANIER, WILLIAM
Virginia, Oregon DAR Daughter

LANNING, JOHN, PVT.
North Carolina, SAR Compatriot George Lanning, Oregon DAR Daughter

LARRICK, CASPER
Virginia, Oregon DAR Daughter

LATHROP, DIXWELL
Connecticut, Oregon DAR Daughter

LAWLESS, AUGUSTINE, CPL.
Virginia, Oregon DAR Daughter

LAWRENCE JONATHAN, PVT.
Massachusetts, Oregon DAR Daughter

LAWSON, JOHN, LT.
Virginia, Oregon DAR Daughter

Lawson, Joseph
Pennsylvania, Oregon DAR Daughter

Lawson, Randolph
North Carolina, Oregon DAR Daughter

Lawton, Joseph
South Carolina, Oregon DAR Daughter

Lay, Thomas
SAR Compatriot Larry Lay

Layport, George, Pvt.
Maryland, Oregon DAR Daughter

Leach, Hezekiah, Pvt.
Connecticut, Oregon DAR Daughter

Leach, Nathan, Pvt.
Massachusetts, Oregon DAR Daughter

Leach, William
Massachusetts, DAR Daughter Sue Glenn

Leach, William, Sr., Pvt.
Massachusetts, Oregon DAR Daughter

Leake, Josiah, Capt.
Virginia, Oregon DAR Daughter

Leavitt, Peter
New Hampshire, Oregon DAR Daughter

Lee, Thomas
DAR Daughter Belle Passi Chapter

Leeds, James, Sgt.
New Jersey, Oregon DAR Daughter

LeFevre, Jacob
Pennsylvania, Oregon DAR Daughter

Leffingwell, Samuel
SAR Compatriot Kenneth Alger

Leigh, Daniel
 New Jersey, Oregon DAR Daughter

Leonard, George
 Pennsylvania, Oregon DAR Daughter

Leonard, Patrick
 SAR Compatriot Jesston Wagner

Leonard, Samuel, QtrMstr.
 Massachusetts, Oregon DAR Daughter

Leonard, Valentine
 North Carolina, Oregon DAR Daughter

Lewis, Jeremiah
 North Carolina, Oregon DAR Daughter

Lewis, Philip
 North Carolina, Oregon DAR Daughter

Lewis, Samuel
 Virginia, Oregon DAR Daughter

Lindsey, Archibald
 SAR Compatriot Fred Heiserman

Linsley, Simeon, Pvt.
 Connecticut, Oregon DAR Daughter

Lippard, John
 North Carolina, Oregon DAR Daughter

Lipscomb, Thomas
 DAR Daughter Betty Mack

Little, Moses, Pvt.
 Massachusetts, DAR Daughter Evelyn Laughman

Little, Thomas
 Virginia, Oregon DAR Daughter

Livermore, Daniel
 Massachusetts, Oregon DAR Daughter

LIVERS, ARNOLD
   Maryland, Oregon DAR Daughter

LIVINGSTON, JAMES
   New York, Oregon DAR Daughter

LOCKWOOD, ABRAHAM, CAPT.
   Rhode Island, Oregon DAR Daughter

LOGAN, JAMES
   Virginia, Oregon DAR Daughter

LOGUE, JOHN, PVT.
   Pennsylvania, Oregon DAR Daughter

LONG, DAVID, PVT.
   Massachusetts, Oregon DAR Daughter

LONG, JOHN, STAFOFF.
   Massachusetts, Oregon DAR Daughter

LONG, JOSEPH, PVT.
   Maryland, Oregon DAR Daughter

LONG, WILLIAM, SR.
   Pennsylvania, Oregon DAR Daughter

LOOMIS, JOHN, ENS.
   Connecticut, Oregon DAR Daughter

LOONEY, PETER
   Virginia, North Carolina, Oregon DAR Daughter

LOUNSBURY, MICHAEL, PVT.
   Connecticut, Oregon DAR Daughter

LOVEWELL, NEHEMIAH, SR., CAPT.
   Vermont, Oregon DAR Daughter

LOVING, GABRIEL, LT.
   North Carolina, Oregon DAR Daughter

LOVINS, ARTHUR
   North Carolina, Oregon DAR Daughter

LOWTHER, WILLIAM
Virginia, Oregon DAR Daughter

LUCAS, WILLIAM, CAPT.
Virginia, Oregon DAR Daughter

LUDLAM, WILLIAM
New York, Oregon DAR Daughter

LYMAN, BENJAMIN, PVT.
Vermont, Oregon DAR Daughter

LYMAN, JOHN
Massachusetts, Oregon DAR Daughter

LYNCH, HENRY
DAR Daughter Belle Passi Chapter

LYON, ISRAEL
New York, Oregon DAR Daughter

LYON, JAMES, LTCOL.
Virginia, Oregon DAR Daughter

LYON, JOHN, LT.
1st Bat. Northumberland Co. Pennsylvania Militia SAR Compatriots Connor Wilson, Christopher Wilson, Oregon DAR Daughter

M

MABIE, HARMANUS, CAPT.
New York, Oregon DAR Daughter

MACLIN, FREDERICK, COL.
Virginia, Oregon DAR Daughter

MACOMBER, ABIEL, LT.
Massachusetts, Oregon DAR Daughter

MACOMBER, JOHN
Massachusetts, Rhode Island, Oregon DAR Daughter

MAHAN, JAMES, PVT.
Virginia, Oregon DAR Daughter

MAHAN, JOHN, LT.
Virginia Continental Line, SAR Compatriots Johnny Alexander, Tyler McClintock

MAINE, JONAS, ENS.
Connecticut, Oregon DAR Daughter

MAJORS, GEORGE
SAR Compatriot Thomas Freedland

MANN, ANDREW, CAPT.
Pennsylvania, Oregon DAR Daughter

MANN, FREDERICK
DAR Daughter Belle Passi Chapter

MANN, JAMES
Georgia, Oregon DAR Daughter

MANVILLE, NICHOLAS
Connecticut, Oregon DAR Daughter

MAPLES, WILLIAM CONDRA
Virginia, Oregon DAR Daughter

MARKHAM, DANIEL, PVT.
Connecticut, Oregon DAR Daughter

MARSH, JOSEPH, PVT.
Massachusetts, Oregon DAR Daughter

MARSHALL, AARON, PVT.
Pennsylvania, Virginia, Oregon DAR Daughter

MARSHALL, EZEKIEL
Virginia, Oregon DAR Daughter

MARSHALL, ISAAC
SAR Compatriots Tom Boardman, Edward Boardman

MARSTELLER, PHILIP, LTCOL.
Paymaster Pennsylvania State Militia 1776-1782

SAR Compatriot Gregory Keller, Oregon DAR Daughter

1776-1782 Philip Marsteller was a delegate to the Pennsylvania Constitutional Convention of 1776 and a member of the state assembly. He was Paymaster of the State Militia and was appointed Lt. Colonel in 1777. He acted as an agent for the French fleet in 1779 and was Assistant Forage Master in 1780 and later named Assistant Deputy Quartermaster General.

He was a personal friend of George Washington and the only non-mason pall bearer at his funeral.

Colonel Marsteller is buried in Christ Church Yard in Alexandria Virginia

MARTIN, ISAAC
SAR Compatriot Jerry Bonnell

MARTIN, JACOB
New Jersey, Oregon DAR Daughter

MARTIN, JOHN, LT.
North Carolina, Oregon DAR Daughter

MARTIN, JOSEPH
Virginia, Oregon DAR Daughter

MASON, GEORGE
Virginia, Oregon DAR Daughter

MASSIA, WILLIAM
DAR Daughter Patti Waitman-Ingebretsen

MATTHEWS, MOSES
South Carolina, Oregon DAR Daughter

MATTHEWS, REUBEN
Connecticut, Oregon DAR Daughter

MATTICE, CONRAD, PVT.
New York, Oregon DAR Daughter

MAXHAM, SAMUEL, PVT.
Massachusetts, Oregon DAR Daughter

MAXWELL, JOHN, CAPT.
Virginia, Oregon DAR Daughter

May, Jacob
Maryland, Oregon DAR Daughter

Mayfield, Henry, Pvt.
Virginia, Oregon DAR Daughter

Mayo, John, Pvt.
Massachusetts, Oregon DAR Daughter

Mayo, Joseph, Sr.
Massachusetts, Oregon DAR Daughter

Mays, Benjamin, Pvt.
Virginia, Oregon DAR Daughter

McBee, Israel
Virginia, Oregon DAR Daughter

McClatchey, George, Pvt.
Pennsylvania, Oregon DAR Daughter

McCleskey, James
Virginia, North Carolina, South Carolina, Oregon DAR Daughter

McClintock, John, Sr.
Pennsylvania, Oregon DAR Daughter

McClintock, William
DAR Daughter Belle Passi Chapter

McConnell, George
Pennsylvania, Oregon DAR Daughter

McCormick, William
Pennsylvania, Oregon DAR Daughter

McCoy, William
SAR Compatriot Robert Bogardus

McCullers, John, Capt.
North Carolina, Oregon DAR Daughter

McCulloch, John, Sr.
Virginia, Oregon DAR Daughter

McDaniel, Robert
Pennsylvania, Oregon DAR Daughter

McDonald, Hugh, NonCom.
South Carolina, Oregon DAR Daughter

McDowell, Joseph
North Carolina, Oregon DAR Daughter

McDowell, Mathew, Pvt.
Pennsylvania, Oregon DAR Daughter

McElnay, John
Pennsylvania, Oregon DAR Daughter

McGee, John
Pennsylvania, Oregon DAR Daughter

McGlathery, Issac
Pennsylvania, Oregon DAR Daughter

McGrew, Patrick
Pennsylvania, Oregon DAR Daughter

McGrew, William
DAR Daughter Belle Passi Chapter

McGrey, James
DAR Daughter Belle Passi Chapter

McKay, Robert, Pvt.
Virginia, Oregon DAR Daughter

McKenny, David
Pennsylvania, Oregon DAR Daughter

McManus, John, Pvt.
Virginia, Oregon DAR Daughter

McNamee, Hugh
Oregon DAR Daughter

McNeely, Hugh
DAR Daughter Belle Passi Chapter

MCNEIL, JOHN
DAR Daughter Belle Passi Chapter

MCNEIL, JONATHAN
Virginia, Oregon DAR Daughter

MCNITT, ALEXANDER, CAPT.
New York, Oregon DAR Daughter

MCNITT, DANIEL, SGT.
New York, Oregon DAR Daughter

MCQUISTON, JAMES
Pennsylvania, Oregon DAR Daughter

MEACHAM, SAMUEL, PVT.
Oregon DAR Daughter

MEANS, ROBERT
North Carolina, Oregon DAR Daughter

MEEKER, JOSEPH
Oregon DAR Daughter

MEISENHEIMER, PETER
SAR Compatriots Willis Meisenheimer, Ricky Meisenheimer, Dean Meisenheimer, Douglas Meisenheimer, Brian Meisenheimer, Patrick Meisenheimer

MELLEN, THOMAS, PVT.
New Hampshire, Oregon DAR Daughter

MELSON, DANIEL
Deleware, Oregon DAR Daughter

MELVIN, JONATHAN, PVT.
Massachusetts, Oregon DAR Daughter

MELVIN, WILLIAM PVT.
Worcester County, Maryland 1778 SAR Compatriots Eugene Melvin, Michael Melvin, Christopher Williams, Oregon DAR Daughter

MEMS, DAVID
Virginia, Oregon DAR Daughter

MENDENHALL, MORDECAI
 North Carolina, DAR Daughter Belle Passi Chapter

MERCER, PETER
 North Carolina, Oregon DAR Daughter

MERCER, THOMAS
 Pennsylvania, Oregon DAR Daughter

MEREDITH, JOHN WHEELER
 Deleware, Oregon DAR Daughter

MERRIFIELD, SAMUEL, SR.
 Virginia, Oregon DAR Daughter

MERRIL, ASHER
 SAR Compatriot Eugene King

MERRIMAN, AMOS
 Connecticut, DAR Daughter Belle Passi Chapter

MERRIMAN, ELISAPH
 Connecticut, Oregon DAR Daughter

MERRIMAN, FREDERICK
 SAR Compatriot Gary Szolomayer

MEYERS, HENRY
 Pennsylvania, Oregon DAR Daughter

MICHENER, MORDECAI
 Pennsylvania, Oregon DAR Daughter

MICKEY, DANIEL, PVT.
 Pennsylvania, Oregon DAR Daughter

MILES, THOMAS, LT.
 North Carolina, Oregon DAR Daughter

MILEY, JOHN HENRY
 Oregon DAR Daughter

MILLER, BENJAMIN, PVT.
 New Jersey, Oregon DAR Daughter

MILLER, FRIEDRICK
DAR Daughter Belle Passi Chapter

MILLER, HENRY, SGT.
North Carolina, Oregon DAR Daughter

MILLER, JOHN
DAR Daughter Patti Waitman-Ingebretsen

MILLER, JAMES, JR.
DAR Daughter Janice Gadway Gardner

MILLIKEN, SAMUEL
Provided supplies to Valley Forge SAR Compatriot Johnny Alexander

MING, WOLRICH
Pennsylvania, Oregon DAR Daughter

MINNICH, WENDEL
Pennsylvania, Oregon DAR Daughter

MITCHELL, ABRAHAM, PVT.
North Carolina, Oregon DAR Daughter

MITCHELL, DAVID
Pennsylvania, Oregon DAR Daughter

MITCHELL, JOHN, SR.
Massachusetts, Oregon DAR Daughter

MITCHELL, WILLIAM
Pennsylvania, Oregon DAR Daughter

MOFFAT, JOSEPH, MD
Massachusetts, Oregon DAR Daughter

MONK, ELIAS
Connecticut, Oregon DAR Daughter

MONK, WILLIAM
Georgia, Oregon DAR Daughter

MONNETT, ABRAHAM
Maryland, Oregon DAR Daughter

MOORE, ABRAHAM
New Hampshire, Oregon DAR Daughter

MOORE, ANDREW
Pennsylvania, Oregon DAR Daughter

MOORE, JONAH
Connecticut, Oregon DAR Daughter

MOORE, JONATHAN, SR.
SAR Compatriot Fred Butcher

MOORE, SAMUEL
New Hampshire, Oregon DAR Daughter

MOORE, THOMAS GUTHRIE, PVT.
Virginia, Oregon DAR Daughter

MORGAN, CHRISTOPHER, ENS.
Connecticut, Oregon DAR Daughter

MORGAN, SOLOMON
South Carolina, Oregon DAR Daughter

MORGAN, TEMPERANCE
Connecticut, Oregon DAR Daughter

MORGAN, WILLIAM
Connecticut, Oregon DAR Daughter

MORLEY, JOHN
Massachusetts, Oregon DAR Daughter

MORRAL, SAMUEL
Virginia, Oregon DAR Daughter

MORRILL, ABRAHAM
New Hampshire, Oregon DAR Daughter

MORRILL, EZEKIEL
New Hampshire, Oregon DAR Daughter

MORRIS, RICHARD
Virginia, Oregon DAR Daughter

MORRISON, JOHN, SR.
New York, Oregon DAR Daughter

MORSE, PETER, PVT.
Massachusetts, DAR Daughter Evelyn Laughman

MOSER, BURKHART, SR.
Pennsylvania, Oregon DAR Daughter

MOSHER, TOBIAS, PVT.
North Carolina, Oregon DAR Daughter

MOSS (MORSE), JOSEPH
Pennsylvania, Oregon DAR Daughter

MOSS, TITUS
Connecticut Line, SAR Compatriot Don Thomas

MOTSINGER (MATZINGER), FELIX
North Carolina, Oregon DAR Daughter

MOULTON, DANIEL
DAR Daughter Belle Passi Chapter

MOUNT, HUMPHREY, PVT.
New Jersey, Oregon DAR Daughter

MOUSER/MUSSER, JOHN
Virginia, Oregon DAR Daughter

MUDGE, JOHN
Massachusetts, Oregon DAR Daughter

MULKEY, JONATHAN
Virginia, Oregon DAR Daughter

MULKEY, PHILLIP, II
North Carolina, Oregon DAR Daughter

MUNGER, JONATHAN, CPL.
Connecticut, Oregon DAR Daughter

MUNGER, NATHAN
Massachusetts, Oregon DAR Daughter

Munn, James
  Massachusetts, Oregon DAR Daughter

Musser, John, Sr.
  Virginia, Oregon DAR Daughter

Muzzey, John
  New Hampshire, Oregon DAR Daughter

Myers, Christopher, Pvt.
  Maryland, Oregon DAR Daughter

Myers, George, Pvt.
  Maryland, Oregon DAR Daughter

Myers, Henry, Ensign
  Pennsylvania, DAR Daughter Patti Waitman-Ingebretsen

Myers, Michael
  Maryland, Oregon DAR Daughter

N

Nantz, Ruben
  Virginia, Oregon DAR Daughter

Nave, Abraham, Pvt.
  North Carolina, Oregon DAR Daughter

Nave, Teter
  North Carolina, Oregon DAR Daughter

Nelson, Henry
  Massachusetts, Oregon DAR Daughter

Nelson, John
  Pennsylvania, Oregon DAR Daughter

Nelson, Josiah
  Massachusetts, Oregon DAR Daughter

Nelson, Nathaniel
  Massachusetts, Oregon DAR Daughter

NEUFANG, BALTHASER
Pennsylvania, Oregon DAR Daughter

NEWHARD, MICHAEL, SEN.
Pennsylvania, Oregon DAR Daughter

NEWMAN, NIMROD
SAR Compatriots Tom Boardman, Ed Boardman

NEWTON, JAMES, PVT.
Massachusetts, Oregon DAR Daughter

NICHOLS, MOSES
Massachusetts, Oregon DAR Daughter

NICKELL, ANDREW
Virginia, Oregon DAR Daughter

NOBLE, STEPHEN
Massachusetts, Oregon DAR Daughter

NONEMACHER, LUDWIG
Pennsylvania, Oregon DAR Daughter

NORTON, NATHAN, SGT.
Vermont, Oregon DAR Daughter

NOYES, BELA
Massachusetts, Oregon DAR Daughter

NURSE, JOSEPH, PVT.
New Hampshire, Oregon DAR Daughter

NUTT, JAMES
Massachusetts, Oregon DAR Daughter

NYE, DAVID, PVT.
Massachusetts, Oregon DAR Daughter

O

OBERLY, JOHN MICHAEL
Pennsylvania, Oregon DAR Daughter

ODELL, JOHN
South Carolina, Oregon DAR Daughter

ODOM, JOHN
North Carolina, Oregon DAR Daughter

OGLESBY, JESSIE
SAR Compatriot Robert Stewart

OHLEN, HENRY GEORGE, SGT.
New York, Oregon DAR Daughter

OLIN, CALEB, ENS.
Vermont, Oregon DAR Daughter

OLIVER, JOHN
DAR Daughter Belle Passi Chapter

OLNEY, JOSEPH, CAPT.
Rhode Island, Oregon DAR Daughter

OVERACKER, ADAM
New York, Oregon DAR Daughter

OVERACKER, MICHAEL
New York, Oregon DAR Daughter

OWEN, DAVID, PVT.
North Carolina, Oregon DAR Daughter

OWEN, THOMAS
SAR Compatriots Dennis Moore, Elijah Moore

P

PACKARD, ROBERT
New Hampshire, Oregon DAR Daughter

PACKER, ELI
Pennsylvania, Oregon DAR Daughter

PAGE, ROBERT, PVT.
Virginia, Oregon DAR Daughter

PAINE, SOLOMON
Connecticut, Oregon DAR Daughter

PAISLEY, THOMAS
Virginia, Oregon DAR Daughter

PALMER, JOHN
New Hampshire DAR Daughter Sue Proud

PALMER, RUFUS
DAR Daughter Belle Passi Chapter

PARISH, WILLIAM, PVT.
Virginia, Oregon DAR Daughter

PARK, AARON
Massachusetts, Oregon DAR Daughter

PARK, THOMAS, CPL.
Connecticut, Oregon DAR Daughter

PARKER, BENJAMIN, PVT.
Vermont, DAR Daughter Evelyn Laughman

PARKER, ELIADA
Connecticut, Oregon DAR Daughter

PARKER, ELISHA, PVT.
Massachusetts, Oregon DAR Daughter

PARKER, GABRIEL
North Carolina, Oregon DAR Daughter

PARKER, HENRY
Oregon DAR Daughter

PARKER, MATTHEW
North Carolina, Oregon DAR Daughter

PARKER, TIMOTHY, CAPT.
Massachusetts, SAR Compatriot Cleve Parker

PARKHURST, MOSES, PVT.
6th Massachusetts Regiment of the Massachusetts Line 1779-1783 SAR Compatriots Michael Tieman, Riley Erwin,

Jackson Erwin, Connor Tieman, Owen Tieman-Woodward

 Age 16 yrs.; stature, 5 ft.4 in.; complexion, light; engaged for town of Mendon; marched July 21, 1779

 Moses PARKHURST was born in Mendon now Milford, Massachusetts in 1762, the son of Samuel PARKHURST and Kezia BEMIS.

 Nothing is known at the moment about Moses' childhood, or what his father did. Was his father, Samuel, a landowner, farmer, shopkeeper, laborer or did he have a craft like a carpenter, or professional occupation like a lawyer?

 In 1779 at age16 Moses enlisted to fight in the American Revolutionary War. He originally enlisted in the 6th Massachusetts Regiment, the Massachusetts Line, commanded by Col. Nixon for nine months. Moses re-enlisted before the end of the term in the same regiment, in the company commanded by Capt. John Holden.

 The 6th Massachusetts Regiment also known as the 4th Continental Regiment was raised on April 23, 1775 under Colonel John Nixon outside of Boston, Massachusetts. The regiment was part of the Massachusetts Line and would see action at the Battle of Bunker Hill, New York Campaign, Battle of Trenton, Battle of Princeton and the Battle of Saratoga. The regiment was furloughed June 12, 1783 at West Point, New York and disbanded on November 3, 1783

 The size of the Massachusetts Line varied from as many as 27 active regiments (at the outset of the war) to four (at its end). For most of the war after the Siege of Boston (April 1775 to March 1776) almost all of these units were deployed outside Massachusetts, serving as far north as Quebec City, as far west as present-day central Upstate New York, and as far south as Yorktown, Virginia. Massachusetts line troops were involved in most of the war's major battles north of Chesapeake Bay, and were present at the decisive Siege of Yorktown in 1781.

 The line's history began in the immediate aftermath of the Battles of Lexington and Concord in April 1775, after which the Massachusetts Provincial Congress raised 27 regiments as a provincial army. These units, which were mostly organized by mid-May, were adopted into the first establishment of the Continental Army in June 1775.

 The Massachusetts Line fought and lived in the Hudson River Valley during Mosses' stay.

 They were camped and patrolled in Westchester County,

Constitution Island, Continental Village, Peekskill, Pines Bridge and Yorktown.

I do not have any letters by Moses and I don't even know if he could write, but there are many journals of men who fought in this area at the same time as Moses, and it was not pretty. Journal entries from 1779-1783 tell of the soldiers being promised new uniforms, daily rations of hot food and water and spirits, ammunition and powder, blankets, beds, tents and in the winter warm cabins. In return, they were fighting and dying for their country.

In reality, they had to stitch together some form of mismatched clothing from what they could find, many did not have shoes, they went days without any food or water unless they could steal some, and when they got rations it would be cold -dried salt cod and hard bread plus some water. At night they slept on the cold ground lacking not only tents, but also in most cases blankets. The winters they had to build their own cabins and scrounge for something to burn to keep warm but the problems of food were worse. Constantly cold, wet, starving and thirsty then we add the daily patrols and guard duty they had to walk, and oh yes the long marches to engage the enemy and then the trek back to camp. This is true dedication to a cause.

Moses was furloughed in in Dec 1782 and honorably discharged in July 1783 at New Windsor, New York. He received his written discharge papers signed by General Washington.

His military record does not show any battles he was in, but he was awarded the badge of merit for three years faithful service and it showed he was paid every 12 months for those three years.

On 11th of October 1787 Moses married Catherine HUCKER, in Franklin, Massachusetts and they had seven children; Horace1788-1833, Nellie 1790-1859, Susanhah 1796-1878, Jotham 1798-1860, Sophia 1800-?, William 1812-?, and Moses Henry (my direct line ancestor) born in Killingly Connecticut in 1820 and died in Keokuk, Iowa in 1881. I do not have any information on Moses' wife except that she died in 1830, but she is not named in his will, only the names of the executers are named and the judge.

This is where the paper trail gets a bit confused.

According to the new Federal government anyone who fought in the Revolutionary War was granted Bounty Land of 100 acres, in a spot designated by Congress.

A 4,000 square mile tract was located in the Northwest

Territory and was set aside for these land warrants. This area came to be known as the U.S. Military District of Ohio. Originally the lands in this district were to be distributed by January 1, 1800. By the end of 1802 about 14,000 warrants had been issued. However, additional time was needed to locate warrants and to grant warrants to soldiers with late applications or uncompleted claims. Congress passed the act of 1803, which was later amended by the act of 1806, to extend the time limit.

The first pension law based on service was passed in 1818, but it was later amended to make eligible only those soldiers unable to earn a living. Fires in 1800 destroyed the earliest Revolutionary War pension application records.

I have papers filed by Moses for his pension in 1818 (30 pages) showing the deed for his Bounty Land 100 acres dated 3 Mar 1803. There is also a deed of sale for that same Bounty Land filed in the state of Massachusetts 6th Jan 1797 by Moses for $20 (farmland sold for around $2/acre at that time) to a Samuel Ide and signed by J. Fisher Justice of the Peace. In 1806another document was filed by Fisher to take away that same Bounty Land from Moses by the courts in Connecticut. When and who owned the land and when it was sold is up for debate I suppose, somewhere there is some more paperwork hopefully clearing this all up.

Anyhow, in 1818 Moses filed for his pension of $8/mo. and got it. In 1820, the federal gov't. changed the pension rules again and only those who fought in the Revolutionary War and could not work were entitled to the pension.

Moses refiled for his pension in 1820, "The applicant is not in good health being constantly affected with jaundice & _____ complaint which renders him unfit for labour, his occupation a common laborer.", and he listed his estate item by item showing he was poor and worth only $21.11 (1 cow worth 15.00 Dolls., 1 goat worth 3.00 Dolls., 3 chairs worth 50 cts, 1 pot 50 cts, 1 dish kettle 30 cts, 1 small skillet 12 cts. 4 cups & saucers 10 cts, 1 broken tea kettle 25cts, 1 hoe 17 cts, 1 pail 10 cts, old casks 17 cts). Moses needed the pension so his family, wife and two sons William aged 8 years and Moses Jr. 4 mos. could live.

At that time, a common laborer when he could work could make $.68/day or $20.40/mo., a carpenter $1/day or $30/mo.and a mason $1.22/day or $36.60/mo.

In the 1820's the Industrial Revolution kicks in and drives

prices and wages down. From 1820-1830 the prices of goods and wages dropped by 50%.

Nothing more is known of Moses and his family until his will was probated 12 Feb 1827 in Connecticut, date also on his pension stop date papers, and his estate was now worth $4.12 in goods and $42.35 in pension cash.

PARKMAN, HENRY, JR., WAGONEER
South Carolina, Oregon DAR Daughter

PARMENTER, ?
DAR Daughter Belle Passi Chapter

PARMENTER, ISAAC, PVT.
Massachusetts, Oregon DAR Daughter

PARMENTER, JEDEDIAH
Massachusetts, Oregon DAR Daughter

PARMENTER, JOSHUA
Massachusetts, Oregon DAR Daughter

PARR, JOHN, SR.
Virginia, Oregon DAR Daughter

PARRISH, HENRY
North Carolina, Oregon DAR Daughter

PARSONS, JOEL
DAR Daughter Belle Passi Chapter

PARTRIDGE, ELISHA
Vermont, Oregon DAR Daughter

PATTERSON, JOHN
North Carolina, Oregon DAR Daughter

PATTERSON, ROBERT
North Carolina, Oregon DAR Daughter

PATTON, JOSEPH
Pennsylvania, Oregon DAR Daughter

PEARSALL, SAMPSON
Pennsylvania, Oregon DAR Daughter

PEASE, EZEKIEL
DAR Daughter Belle Passi Chapter

PECK, ABEL
Connecticut, Oregon DAR Daughter

PECK, EHPRAIM
Connecticut, Oregon DAR Daughter

PECK, GEORGE, PVT.
Virginia, Oregon DAR Daughter

PECKHAM, JONATHAN, PVT.
Massachusetts, Oregon DAR Daughter

PEDIGO, EDWARD
Virginia, Oregon DAR Daughter

PEMBERTON, PATRICK GRANT
Connecticut, Oregon DAR Daughter

PENCE, HENRY
Oregon DAR Daughter

PENINGER, HENRY
Virginia, Oregon DAR Daughter

PENNEY, JOHN, PVT.
Massachusetts, Oregon DAR Daughter

PENNIMAN, PETER
Massachusetts, Oregon DAR Daughter

PENNYPACK, WILLIAM, PVT.
Pennsylvania, Oregon DAR Daughter

PERKINS, THOMAS
Massachusetts, Oregon DAR Daughter

PERLEY, ASA
Massachusetts, Oregon DAR Daughter

PERLEY, DUDLEY, LT.
Massachusetts, Oregon DAR Daughter

PETERS, CASPER, SR.
Pennsylvania, Oregon DAR Daughter

PHELPS, NORMAN
Connecticut, Oregon DAR Daughter

PHILLIPS, ASA, PVT.
Connecticut, Oregon DAR Daughter

PHILLIPS, ESQUIRE, PVT.
Connecticut, Oregon DAR Daughter

PHILLIPS, LOT, PVT.
Ney Jersey, Oregon DAR Daughter

PHILLIS, JOSEPH, PVT.
Pennsylvania, Oregon DAR Daughter

PHIPPS, SAMUEL, PVT.
Pennsylvania, Oregon DAR Daughter

PICKENS, ROBERT MASON
North Carolina, Oregon DAR Daughter

PICKLE, MATHIAS
SAR Compatriot Gene Lambird

PIERCE, CALEB, NONCOM
Massachusetts, Rhode Island, Oregon DAR Daughter

PIERCE, JAMES
Pennsylvania, Oregon DAR Daughter

PIERPONT, EVELYN, LT.
Connecticut, Oregon DAR Daughter

PINNEO, JAMES, CAPT.
Connecticut, Oregon DAR Daughter

PINNEO, JOSEPH, PVT.
Connecticut, Oregon DAR Daughter

PINNEY, FRANCES
SAR Compatriot Jack Pinney

PIRKLE, JOHN JACOB
North Carolina, Oregon DAR Daughter

PIPPEN, JOHN
North Carolina, Oregon DAR Daughter

PITMAN, JONATHAN
New Jersey DAR Daughter Janis Allen

PLAISTED, SAMUEL
DAR Daughter Belle Passi Chapter

POLK, CHARLES
Virginia, Oregon DAR Daughter

POLK, CHARLES, CAPT.
North Carolina, Oregon DAR Daughter

POLLOCK, JOHN, PVT.
Pennsylvania, Oregon DAR Daughter

POMEROY, DANIEL, PVT.
Connecticut, Oregon DAR Daughter

POOL, SAMUEL, JR.
Massachusetts, Oregon DAR Daughter

POORMAN, DANIEL, PVT.
Pennsylvania, Oregon DAR Daughter

POPE, CHRISTOPHER
DAR Daughter Belle Passi Chapter

PORTER, ELIZABETH DUNKIN
Oregon DAR Daughter

PORTER, HUGH
DAR Daughter Betty Mack

PORTER, MOSES
Connecticut, Oregon DAR Daughter

PORTER, WILLIAM, LTCOL.
Rutherford Militia North Carolina 1776-1782 SAR Compatriots Eric Salbeda, Kade Salbeda, Ian Salbeda, Aidan Christensen

William Porter was born in Lancaster Pennsylvania around 1746. He was the son of James and Nancy Porter who immigrated from Donegal, Ireland. In 1768 the family moved to North Carolina, and settled in Tryon County, later renamed Rutherford County.

Gilbertown served as the county seat and the early town records shows William Porter was in attendance at the first session of the County Court.

He was noted as being "a man of great influence both in his church and county". William also served as an elder at Britain Presbyterian Church, the oldest such house of worship in Rutherford County. William Porter served in the militia as a Captain under the overall command of Brigadier General Griffith Rutherford, for whom the town of Rutherfordton was named.

During the Revolutionary War, frontier settlers who opposed British rule were harassed by both Indians and Tories. The Cherokee had formed an alliance with Britain, were heavily supplied with arms, and ordered by British agents to attack Patriot towns and homesteads.

Alexander Dunn, in his 1802 pension file, (R3142) recounts:

April 1779, was drafted for three months tour of service, in Rutherford County, North Carolina, he was mustered into service under Captain William Porter. The company marched to and was stationed in Mumford's Cove at Archibold's Grants. This company was called into service to guard against the Cherokee Indians who had committed repeated deputations.

With his tour of duty complete, William Porter became a Senator in 1780. However, his legislative duties would be delayed for a time due to the British Invasion of North Carolina. He was recalled under the command of Colonel Joseph McDowell to prepare the Rutherford militia for the upcoming battle against Major Patrick Ferguson, the British officer commanding the western flank of Lord Cornwallis's army.

After a rendezvous with the "Overmountain Men" of Tennessee, they attacked and defeated Ferguson and his Loyalist militia on October 7, 1780 at the Battle of Kings Mountain.

Fighting alongside William Porter was his brother, Major James Porter; and also their cousin, Lieutenant Colonel Robert Porter.

James was wounded in battle and subsequently removed to Greenville County, South Carolina where he recovered from his wounds.

The Patriot victory at King's Mountain was one of the turning points in the Southern theater of the Revolutionary War as it temporarily forced Lord Cornwallis to abandon his invasion of North Carolina, and allowed more time for the Patriots to gather their forces.

POTTER, AMOS
New Jersey, Oregon DAR Daughter

POTTER, RUSSELL
New Jersey, Oregon DAR Daughter

POTTER, THOMAS
DAR Daughter Belle Passi Chapter

POTTS, WILLIAM
New Jersey, Oregon DAR Daughter

POWELL, JOSEPH PVT.
North Carolina, Oregon DAR Daughter

POWELL, LEVIN
Virginia, Oregon DAR Daughter

POWELL, MOSES, PVT.
North Carolina, Oregon DAR Daughter

POWELL, WILLIAM, PVT.
Pennsylvania, Oregon DAR Daughter

POWERS, GIDEON
Massachusetts, Maine, Oregon DAR Daughter

PRATER, ZACHARIAH
SAR Compatriots Jeffrey Claxton, Aaron Claxton, Stefan Claxton

PRATHER, THOMAS, PVT.
North Carolina, Oregon DAR Daughter

PRESCOTT, JEDEDIAH
New Hampshire, Oregon DAR Daughter

PRESCOTT, TIMOTHY
Massachusetts, Oregon DAR Daughter

PRICE, SAMUEL
Connecticut, Oregon DAR Daughter

PRICE, WILLIAM , JR. 1ST LT.
Command detachment 3rd Artillery Reg., Cambridge, Mass, May 3, 1775 SAR Compatriot D. Price

PRUYN, FRANCIS
Oregon DAR Daughter

PUCKETT, DRURY PVT.
Virginia, Oregon DAR Daughter

PULLEN, STEPHEN
Massachusetts, Oregon DAR Daughter

PULSIPHER, DAVID
SAR Compatriot Earl Wiest

PUTNAM, ISRAEL
Massachusetts, Oregon DAR Daughter

PUTNAM, PHINEAS
Massachusetts, Oregon DAR Daughter

Q

QUINTON, SAMUEL
South Carolina, Oregon DAR Daughter

R

RAGLAND, BENJAMIN
SAR Compatriot George Tanner

RAMEY, JACOB, JR.
Virginia, Oregon DAR Daughter

RAMEY, JACOB, SR.
Virginia, Oregon DAR Daughter

Ramey, James, Pvt.
Virginia, Oregon DAR Daughter

Rankin, James, Pvt.
Pennsylvania, Oregon DAR Daughter

Ransom, Samuel
Connecticut, Oregon DAR Daughter

Rawson, Silas
DAR Daughter Belle Passi Chapter

Ray, Andrew
Virginia, Oregon DAR Daughter

Ray, Samuel
Pennsylvania, Oregon DAR Daughter

Rayl, Samuel
SAR Compatriots Christian Mammen, Donald Mammen

Raymer, Frederick
New York, Oregon DAR Daughter

Reagan, Charles, Ens.
Virginia, Oregon DAR Daughter

Record, Josiah, Capt.
DAR Daughter Patti Waitman-Ingebretsen

Record, Seth
Massachusetts, Oregon DAR Daughter

Redfearn, John
Provided goods/services to the cause SAR Compatriot Neil Verigan
WHERE THE RED FERNS GREW
The family sprang from York and Lancaster, and was identified in records as early as 1238. Spelled in a variety of ways, the first member to arrive in the new world was apparently Nicholas Redferne who appeared in Virginia, 1658.

It seems he left no descendants, and no further paper trail. This, however, is about James and John Redfearn (brothers, and Thomas and Robert Huntley.

They weren't among the powerful or wealthy; just small

independent farmers who came to America looking for greater opportunities.

For SAR purposes, I traced my ancestry to John, whose father, James, was born in Virginia around 1735. Moving into North Carolina, John was born before 1755 in Anson County.

Available records show that John provided goods or services to the cause, while brother James was a Revolutionary soldier. Original Revolutionary Army Accounts & Vouchers, Historical Commission,

Raleigh, N.C., have entries showing John with currency allowances of 3 pounds 18 shillings; 11 pounds 4 shillings; and interest of 3 pounds 6 shillings. It isn't clear, however, whether the money was for military service or other services. Auditors for the claims included John Auld, an army officer from Anson County and Thomas Chiles, a captain, from the same county.
John's brother James, mentioned above, while not a direct ancestor, was a Revolutionary soldier.

Pension records show he served in Capt. James White's company of Col. Thomas Wade's regiment.

This would have been in North Carolina, but date of enlistment and length of service aren't included.

His pension began September 5, 1808 at $3.00 per month, and was later raised to $4.80. The last payment was made September 13, 1826. He never married, and lived with his nephew, Nimrod Redfearn, during his later years.

Nimrod was John's son, and my great-great-great-grandfather. His marriage to Sarah Huntley added two other Revolutionary connections to my family tree. Her grandfather, Thomas Huntley, furnished money and materials as evidenced by several pages of Army Records of N.C. And her father, Robert Huntley, was a soldier, referred to in old age as Grandsir Bob. An account of his death at 93 in the June 24, 1854, issue of the "Pee Dee Star" comments that "he was a soldier in the great struggle of his country for independence--was placed as a guard in the battle of Camden when Gates was defeated--afterward aided as one of a scouting party to subdue Tories," etc.

These are my links with our Revolutionary history through my mother, Georgia (Redfearn) Verigan.

My hometown is Monmouth, Illinois, Wyatt Earp's birthplace.

REDMAN, BENJAMIN PVT.
4th Co., Middle Battalion, Militia of Maryland. SAR Compatriots Curtis Loop, Derek Loop, Levi Loop, Thomas Akers, Oregon DAR Daughter
Patriot's Service and Dates: 4th Company (commanded by CPT William Moore), Middle Battalion (commanded by COL Archibald Orme), of the Montgomery County Militia of Maryland. Served under Gen. George Washington in Valley Forge. Was also a Private in the War of 1812

REDUS, JAMES, PVT.
Maryland, and Pennsylvania, Oregon DAR Daughter

REED, ELNATHAN
Massachusetts, Oregon DAR Daughter

REED, JEREMIAH
Pennsylvania, Oregon DAR Daughter

REED, JOHN, CAPT.
New Jersey, Oregon DAR Daughter

REED, JOSEPH
Massachusetts, Oregon DAR Daughter

REED, JOSHUA, PVT.
Virginia, Pennsylvania, Oregon DAR Daughter

REED, JOSHUA
Massachusetts, Oregon DAR Daughter

REITLEHOVER, GEORGE MICHAEL
South Carolina, Oregon DAR Daughter

RENCH, JOSEPH
Maryland, Oregon DAR Daughter

RENFREW, MARK
Virginia, Oregon DAR Daughter

REQUA, GLADE
New York, Oregon DAR Daughter

Reuben, Cook
North Carolina, Oregon DAR Daughter

Reynolds, Stephen
Massachusetts, Oregon DAR Daughter

Rhodes, James
Rhode Island, Oregon DAR Daughter

Rice, Nicholas
Virginia, Oregon DAR Daughter

Richardson, Isaac, Pvt.
Massachusetts, Oregon DAR Daughter

Richardson, Moses
Massachusetts, Oregon DAR Daughter

Rickabaugh, Adam
Virginia, Oregon DAR Daughter

Rickard, Abner
Massachusetts, Oregon DAR Daughter

Rife, Jacob, Pvt.
3rd & 5th Bat. Lancaster Co., Pennsylvania 1778-1783
SAR Compatriot Arlen Clark

Riggs, Edmond
DAR Daughter Belle Passi Chapter

Riggs, James, Pvt.
Lt. Rose's Ranging Co. Pennsylvania SAR Compatriot Jeff Barker

Riggs, Jeremiah Ellis
Pennsylvania, Oregon DAR Daughter

Riley, Ninian
Maryland, Oregon DAR Daughter

Ringo, Cornelius
SAR Compatriot Robert Ringo

Ritchie, Francis
Virginia, Oregon DAR Daughter

RITTER, MARTIN
   Pennsylvania, Oregon DAR Daughter

ROBB, JAMES
   South Carolina, Oregon DAR Daughter

ROBBINS, BRINTNAL, ENS.
   Connecticut, Oregon DAR Daughter

ROBBINS, WILLIAM, PVT.
   North Carolina, Oregon DAR Daughter

ROBERTS, EDWARD
   DAR Daughter Belle Passi Chapter

ROBERTS, JANE
   Virginia, Oregon DAR Daughter

ROBERTS, JOHN
   Virginia, Oregon DAR Daughter

ROBERTS, OWEN MAURICE, COL.
   South Carolina, Oregon DAR Daughter

ROBERTS, RICHARD BROOK
   South Carolina, Oregon DAR Daughter

ROBERTSON, DANIEL, PVT.
   Virginia, Oregon DAR Daughter

ROBERTSON, GEORGE
   Maryland, Oregon DAR Daughter

ROBERTSON, RICHARD
   North Carolina, Oregon DAR Daughter

ROBERTS, OWEN MAURICE, COL.
   South Carolina, Oregon DAR Daughter

ROBISON, JAMES
   New York, Oregon DAR Daughter

ROBINSON, JOHN, PVT.
   New Hampshire, Oregon DAR Daughter

RODEBAUGH, JOHN
Virginia, Oregon DAR Daughter

RODMAN, JOSEPH, PVT.
New York, Oregon DAR Daughter

ROGERS, BENJAMIN
Massachusetts, Oregon DAR Daughter

ROGERS, JOSIAH, PVT.
Connecticut, Oregon DAR Daughter

ROGERS, LEMUEL
Connecticut, Oregon DAR Daughter

ROSE, LEMUEL
Oregon DAR Daughter

ROSE, TIMOTHY, PVT.
Connecticut, Oregon DAR Daughter

ROTH, JONATHAN
Pennsylvania, Oregon DAR Daughter

ROUNDY, URIAH, PVT.
Vermont, Oregon DAR Daughter

ROUSE, SIMEON, PVT.
Massachusetts, Oregon DAR Daughter

ROUSH, GEORGE, PVT.
Virginia, Oregon DAR Daughter

ROZIER, REUBEN
North Carolina, Oregon DAR Daughter

RUGGLES, LEMUEL, PVT.
Massachusetts, Oregon DAR Daughter

RUCH, LORENTZ, PVT.
Pennsylvania, Oregon DAR Daughter

RUGH, JOHN PETER, MAJ.
Pennsylvania, Oregon DAR Daughter

RUSSELL, ANDREW
Pennsylvania, Oregon DAR Daughter

RUSSELL, GEORGE
New Hampshire, Oregon DAR Daughter

RUSSELL, SETH
Massachusetts, Oregon DAR Daughter

RUST, GERSHAM, SGT.
Massachusetts, Oregon DAR Daughter

RUTLEDGE, EDWARD
SAR Compatriot George Lanning

RUYLE, HENRY
Virginia, Oregon DAR Daughter

RYLAND, JOHN
Pennsylvania, Oregon DAR Daughter

S

SALYER, ZACHEUS, PVT.
Capt. Hick's Co. 1st New York Reg. SAR Compatriot Arlen Clark

SAMPSON, JACOB
Massachusetts, Oregon DAR Daughter

SAMS, JONAS
Pennsylvania, Oregon DAR Daughter

SANDES, HENRY, PVT.
South Carolina, Oregon DAR Daughter

SANFORD, EZRA
New York, Oregon DAR Daughter

SANFORD, OLIVER
Vermont, Oregon DAR Daughter

SANTEE, VALENTINE
Pennsylvania, Oregon DAR Daughter

SARGENT, DIAMOND, PVT.
Massachusetts, Oregon DAR Daughter

SAVAGE, JAMES
Massachusetts, Oregon DAR Daughter

SAVITZ, GEORGE
North Carolina, Oregon DAR Daughter

SAWIN, EZEKIEL, PVT.
Massachusetts, Oregon DAR Daughter

SAWYER, AARON
Massachusetts, Oregon DAR Daughter

SAWYER, BENJAMIN
SAR Compatriot Ivon Young

SAWYER, ENOCh
New Hampshire, Oregon DAR Daughter

SCHAEFFER, ANTHONY, PVT.
Pennsylvania, Oregon DAR Daughter

SCHELL, JOHANNES CASPER
North Carolina, Oregon DAR Daughter

SCHENCK, JOHN, CAPT.
New Jersey, Oregon DAR Daughter

SCHLEPPI, JOHANNES
DAR Daughter Belle Passi Chapter

SCHOCK, JOHN, PVT.
Pennsylvania, Oregon DAR Daughter

SCHUCK, PHILLIP
Pennsylvania, Oregon DAR Daughter

SCHWARTZ, GEORGE
Pennsylvania, Oregon DAR Daughter

SCOTHORN, ELIZABETH BROWN
Oregon DAR Daughter

SCOTT, JAMES, LT.
Virginia, Oregon DAR Daughter

SCOTT, JOHN
Virginia, Oregon DAR Daughter

SCOTT, THOMAS
North Carolina, Oregon DAR Daughter

SCRANTON, TIMOTHY, PVT.
Connecticut, Oregon DAR Daughter

SCRIBNER, LEVI
Connecticut, Oregon DAR Daughter

SCROGGINS, HUMPHREY
Virginia, Oregon DAR Daughter

SEAMANS, HEZEKIAH, PVT.
Rhode Island, Oregon DAR Daughter

SEARS, NATHAN
Massachusetts, Oregon DAR Daughter

SEARS, RICHARD, SGT.
Massachusetts, Oregon DAR Daughter

SEAVER, DANIEL, PVT.
Massachusetts, Oregon DAR Daughter

SEAVER, MOSES, PVT.
Massachusetts, Oregon DAR Daughter

SEEBER, SAFFRENESS
New York, Oregon DAR Daughter

SEITZ, PETER
North Carolina, Oregon DAR Daughter

SELKIRK, JAMES, SGT.
New York, Oregon DAR Daughter

SELTZER, JACOB
Pennsylvania, Oregon DAR Daughter

Seltzer, Michael, Pvt.
Pennsylvania, Oregon DAR Daughter

Settle, Reuben
Virginia, Oregon DAR Daughter

Sevier, John, Col.
North Carolina, Oregon DAR Daughter

Seymour, Aaron
Connecticut, Oregon DAR Daughter

Shackelford, Henry
Virginia, Oregon DAR Daughter

Shaklee, Peter, Pvt.
Pennsylvania, Oregon DAR Daughter

Shallenberger, John
Pennsylvania, Oregon DAR Daughter

Shanks, Thomas
Pennsylvania, Oregon DAR Daughter

Sharp, Isaac
Virginia, Oregon DAR Daughter

Sharp, Jacob, Pvt.
New York, Oregon DAR Daughter

Shattuck, Job, Capt.
Massachusetts, Oregon DAR Daughter

Shattuck, Sarah Hartwell
Massachusetts, Oregon DAR Daughter

Shears, Andrew
DAR Daughter Belle Passi Chapter

Sheldon, James, Sr.
Pennsylvania, Oregon DAR Daughter

Sheldon, James
SAR Compatriots Clayton Springermann, Travis Springermann, Marshall Goodwin

SHELLY, DANIEL, PVT.
York Co., Pennsylvania SAR Compatriot Arlen Clark

SHEPARD, ELISHA
SAR Compatriot Henry Winsor

SHEPARD, JAMES
Connecticut, SAR Compatriots John Glen, Jacob Glen, Mason Glen, Oregon DAR Daughter

SHEPARD, ROBERT
North Carolina, Oregon DAR Daughter

SHEPARD, TIMOTHY
Connecticut, Oregon DAR Daughter

SHEPARDSON, JOHN
Virginia, Oregon DAR Daughter

SHEPPARD, CHARLTON
New Jersey, Oregon DAR Daughter

SHERMAN, EBER
Rhode Island, Oregon DAR Daughter

SHERMAN, JOHN, SR.
North Carolina, Oregon DAR Daughter

SHERMAN, RODGER
Connecticut, Oregon DAR Daughter

SHERWOOD, ABEL
Connecticut, Oregon DAR Daughter

SHIELDS, WILLIAM, CAPT.
Maryland, Oregon DAR Daughter

SHIPMAN, ABRAHAM
DAR Daughter Belle Passi Chapter

SHIVE, GEORGE
Pennsylvania, Oregon DAR Daughter

SHOEMAKER, JOHN GEORGE, PVT.
Pennsylvania, Oregon DAR Daughter

SHUFORD, JOHN
North Carolina, Oregon DAR Daughter

SILL, JABEZ, JR., PVT.
Connecticut, Oregon DAR Daughter

SIMMONS, FREDERICK
New York, Oregon DAR Daughter

SIMONS, ADRIEL
Connecticut, Oregon DAR Daughter

SINGLETON, RICHARD, PVT.
South Carolina, Oregon DAR Daughter

SKELTON, JOHN, ENSIGN
DAR Daughter Patti Waitman-Ingebretsen

SKIDMORE, JAMES
Virginia, Oregon DAR Daughter

SKIDMORE, JOHN, CAPT.
Virginia, Oregon DAR Daughter

SKINNER, ELI
Massachusetts, Oregon DAR Daughter

SLADE, PELEG, LTCOL.
Massachusetts, Oregon DAR Daughter

SLAUGHTER, OWEN, SR.
North Carolina, Oregon DAR Daughter

SMALL, ELISHA EDWARD
Massachusetts, Oregon DAR Daughter

SMALL, MATTHEW
Virginia, Oregon DAR Daughter

SMALL, MICAH, PVT.
Massachusetts, DAR Daughter Sue Glenn

SMITH, ANDERSON
North Carolina, Oregon DAR Daughter

SMITH, DOWNING RUCKER
Virginia, Oregon DAR Daughter

SMITH, EDWARD
New Hampshire, Oregon DAR Daughter

SMITH, HENRY
Virginia, Oregon DAR Daughter

SMITH, ISRAEL, CAPT.
Massachusetts, Oregon DAR Daughter

SMITH, JACOB, PVT.
Maryland, Oregon DAR Daughter

SMITH, JOSEPH
Massachusetts, DAR Daughter Sue Glenn

SMITH, MOSES
South Caroli, Oregon DAR Daughter

SMITH, NATHAN
Massachusetts, Oregon DAR Daughter

SNOW, BERNICE
Massachusetts, Oregon DAR Daughter

SNOW, JOHN
New Hampshire, Oregon DAR Daughter

SNOW, SAMUEL
Massachusetts, Oregon DAR Daughter

SNOW, THOMAS, PVT.
Massachusetts, DAR Daughter Sue Glenn

SOBLET (SUBLETT), BENJAMIN, CPL.
Virginia, Oregon DAR Daughter

SOLLERS, THOMAS, MAJ.
Maryland, Oregon DAR Daughter

SOULE, JAMES
Massachusetts, Oregon DAR Daughter

SOUTHMAYD, WILLIAM, SGT.
Connecticut, Oregon DAR Daughter

SOWERS, PAUL
Pennsylvania, Oregon DAR Daughter

SPEAR, JONATHAN, CAPT.
Massachusetts, Oregon DAR Daughter

SPEARS, CHRISTIAN
Virginia, Oregon DAR Daughter

SPEARS, GEORGE F., PVT.
Virginia, Oregon DAR Daughter

SPENCER, ELAM, PVT.
Connecticut, Oregon DAR Daughter

SPRAGUE, HEZEKIAH
Rhode Island, Oregon DAR Daughter

SPRANKEL, MICHAEL
Pennsylvania, Oregon DAR Daughter

SPRANKEL, PETER, SR.
Pennsylvania, Oregon DAR Daughter

SPRINGER, PHILIP
Pennsylvania, Oregon DAR Daughter

SPROUL, ROBERT
Massachusetts, Oregon DAR Daughter

SPROUL, WILLIAM
Massachusetts, Oregon DAR Daughter

SPURGEON/SPURGIN, JAMES
Pennsylvania, Oregon DAR Daughter

STACKHOUSE, JOHN, PVT.
Pennsylvania, Oregon DAR Daughter

STANDISH, SHADRACK, DRM.
Massachusetts, Oregon DAR Daughter

STANFORD, MOSES PVT.
Massachusetts, Oregon DAR Daughter

STANFORD, RICHARD, PVT.
Massachusetts, Oregon DAR Daughter

STAPLES, ISAAC, PVT.
Massachusetts, Oregon DAR Daughter

STAPLES, NATHANIEL, PVT.
Massachusetts, Oregon DAR Daughter

STARBUCK, MATTHEW
Massachusetts, Oregon DAR Daughter

STARK, DANIEL, SR.
Connecticut, Oregon DAR Daughter

STARKWEATHER, JOHN, SGT.
Connecticut, Oregon DAR Daughter

STARLING, ADAM
North Carolina, Oregon DAR Daughter

STEARNS, LEVI, SGT.
Connecticut, Oregon DAR Daughter

STEARNS, PETER
New Hampshire, Oregon DAR Daughter

STECKEL, PETER
Pennsylvania, Oregon DAR Daughter

STEELE, BRADFORD, SR., CAPT.
Connecticut, Oregon DAR Daughter

STEMPLE, GODFREY
Maryland, Oregon DAR Daughter

STEPHENS, GILBERT, PVT.
Virginia, Oregon DAR Daughter

STEVENS, JOSEPH, CPL.
New York, Oregon DAR Daughter

Stevens, Thomas, Pvt.
Maryland, Oregon DAR Daughter

Stevenson, James
Pennsylvania, Oregon DAR Daughter

Stewart, Alexander, Pvt.
Virginia, Oregon DAR Daughter

Stewart, John
Pennsylvania, Oregon DAR Daughter

Stewart, John, Sr.
New Jersey, Oregon DAR Daughter

Stocker, Andreas, Pvt.
Pennsylvania, Oregon DAR Daughter

Stockwell, David
New Hampshire, Oregon DAR Daughter

Stoddard, David
Vermont, Oregon DAR Daughter

Stolp, Peter
New York, Oregon DAR Daughter

Stone, John, Pvt.
Massachusetts DAR Daughter Janice Gadway Gardner

Stone, Moses, Jr.
SAR Compatriot Anthony Stone

Stoner, David
Pennsylvania, Oregon DAR Daughter

Stotts, Solomon
SAR Compatriot Fred Butcher

Stow, Elihu, Jr., Pvt.
Connecticut, Oregon DAR Daughter

Stowell, David
Massachusetts, Oregon DAR Daughter

STRAWN, ISAIAH
 DAR Daughter Belle Passi Chapter

STRAWN, JACOB
 Pennsylvania, Oregon DAR Daughter

STRONG, JOSIAH, PVT.
 Connecticut, Oregon DAR Daughter

STURTEVANT, JESSE, LT.
 Massachusetts, Oregon DAR Daughter

SUBLETT, BENJAMIN, CPL.
 Virginia, Oregon DAR Daughter

SUTHERLAND, WILLIAM
 Virginia, Oregon DAR Daughter

SUTTON, JOHN B., PVT.
 North Carolina, South Carolina, Oregon DAR Daughter

SWEET, SYLVESTER
 Massachusetts, Oregon DAR Daughter

SWEETSER, JOHN, LT.
 Massachusetts, Oregon DAR Daughter

SWIFT, FLOWER, CAPT.
 Virginia, Oregon DAR Daughter

SWIGERT, PHILIP, PVT.
 Pennsylvania, Oregon DAR Daughter

T

TAFT, CALEB
 Massachusetts, Oregon DAR Daughter

TALIFERRO, CRAIG
 Virginia, Oregon DAR Daughter

TAVENNER, GEORGE
 Virginia, Oregon DAR Daughter

TAYLOR, OTHNIEL, SR.
Massachusetts, Oregon DAR Daughter

TEMPLE, JOSEPH, PVT.
Massachusetts, Oregon DAR Daughter

TEMPLE, SOLOMON
Massachusetts, Oregon DAR Daughter

TENNEY, JOHN, PVT.
New Hampshire, Oregon DAR Daughter

TERRELL, EDMUND, CAPT.
Virginia, Oregon DAR Daughter

TERRELL, JOSIAH, CAPT.
Connecticut, Oregon DAR Daughter

TERRY, PARSHALL, PVT.
24th Regiment Connecticut Militia 1776-1778 SAR Compatriot Gary Keyser
    Militiaman at the Continental Post in Wilkes-Barre under Col. Zebulas Butler.
    In 1778, when Butler heard of the destruction caused by the invading Tories and Indians, he decided to assemble his men at Forty Fort, to undertake the defense. Parshall Terry also took part in the battle of Forty-Fort, and is named among about sixty refugees at Forty Fort. Nearly 230 American soldiers were killed and the result of Forty-Fort action ended in 'The Wyoming massacre' which became an important propaganda tool for the patriot cause and also forced Washington to appoint Major General John Sullivan to lead a campaign against the Iroquois on the Pennsylvania and New York Frontier in 1779.
    Parshall Terry died 15 May, 1811 at Tarrytown, Bradford, Pennsylvania.

THOMAS, ALEXANDER
New Jersey, Oregon DAR Daughter

THOMAS, SIMON
North Carolina, Oregon DAR Daughter

THOMAS, WILLIAM, STAFF OFFICER
Massachusetts, Oregon DAR Daughter

THOMPSON, BENAJAH
SAR Compatriot Robert Henry

THOMPSON, ROBERT
New York, Oregon DAR Daughter

THOMPSON, SAMUEL
DAR Daughter Belle Passi Chapter

THOMPSON, THADDEUS, PVT.
Connecticut, Oregon DAR Daughter

THRASH, VALENTINE
North Carolina, Oregon DAR Daughter

THRELKELD, JOHN, PVT.
Virginia, Oregon DAR Daughter

THURSTON, DAVID, PVT.
New Jersey, Oregon DAR Daughter

TICKNOR, DANIEL
Massachusetts, Oregon DAR Daughter

TILGHMAN, JOSHUA
North Carolina, Oregon DAR Daughter

TILLER, JOHN
Virginia, Oregon DAR Daughter

TILLEY, LAZARUS
North Carolina, Oregon DAR Daughter

TILLSON, WILLIAM, PVT
North Carolina, Oregon DAR Daughter

TIMMONS, NEHEMIAH
Maryland, Oregon DAR Daughter

TINDALL, WILLIAM
New Jersey, Oregon DAR Daughter

TINDER, JAMES
SAR Compatriot Stephen Cunliffe

Tingley, Lemuel
New Jersey, Oregon DAR Daughter

Tipps, Jacob
North Carolina, Oregon DAR Daughter

Todd, Jonah
Connecticut, Oregon DAR Daughter

Tofflemire, Martin
DAR Daughter Belle Passi Chapter

Tolman, Benjamin
Pennsylvania, Oregon DAR Daughter

Tompkins, Gideon, Pvt.
Rhode Island, Oregon DAR Daughter

Tower, Nathaniel, Cpl.
Vermont, Oregon DAR Daughter

Trickey, John, Sr.
New Hampshire, Oregon DAR Daughter

Trimble, James
Virginia, Oregon DAR Daughter

Troutman, John
SAR Compatriot Gregory Nelson

Trowbridge, Edmund, Sgt.
Massachusetts, Oregon DAR Daughter

Troxell, Daniel, Pvt.
Pennsylvania, Oregon DAR Daughter

Troxell, Peter, Sr.
Pennsylvania, Oregon DAR Daughter

Trumbell, David
Connecticut, Oregon DAR Daughter

Tubbes, George
North Carolina, Oregon DAR Daughter

Tucker, Ephraim
New Jersey, Oregon DAR Daughter

Tucker, John, Pvt.
Pennsylvania, Oregon DAR Daughter

Tune, Travis
Virginia, Oregon DAR Daughter

Turner, Kerenhappuch
Virginia, Oregon DAR Daughter

Turner, Meshack
Virginia, Oregon DAR Daughter

Turner, William, Pvt.
Virginia, Oregon DAR Daughter

Turney, Adam, Ens.
Pennsylvania, Oregon DAR Daughter

Tuthill, Samuel
Committee to form Union of Colonies, Morris Co. New Jersey SAR Compatriots Johnny Alexander,

Tuttle, Sylvanus
New Jersey, Oregon DAR Daughter

Tyler, Samuel
Connecticut, Oregon DAR Daughter

U

Underhill, Israel
New York, Oregon DAR Daughter

Underhill, John
North Carolina, Oregon DAR Daughter

Utter, Abraham, Pvt.
Pennsylvania, Oregon DAR Daughter

V

VANCE, PATRICK
Pennsylvania, Oregon DAR Daughter

VAN CLEAVE, BENJAMIN
North Carolina, Oregon DAR Daughter

VAN DEUSEN, MATTHEW, CPL.
New York, Oregon DAR Daughter

VAN METER, JACOB, SR.
Virginia, Oregon DAR Daughter

VAN METER, JACOB
Pennsylvania, Oregon DAR Daughter

VAN NESS, PETER
New Jersey, Oregon DAR Daughter

VANNOSDALL, OAKEY, PVT.
New Jersey, SAR Compatriot Arlen Clark

VAN SLYKE, HARMANUS
New York, Oregon DAR Daughter

VAN TASSEL, ABRAHAM
SAR Compatriot Donald Sass Tyler McClintock

VAN WORMER, JACOB, LT.
New York, Oregon DAR Daughter

VARS, ISAAC
Rhode Island, Oregon DAR Daughter

VARNES (WERNS; WERNTZ), GEORGE, ENS.
Pennsylvania, Oregon DAR Daughter

VEEDER, VOLKERT
DAR Daughter Belle Passi Chapter

VENABLE, CHARLES
Virginia, Oregon DAR Daughter

VERNON, RICHARD
Virginia, Oregon DAR Daughter

VERNON, RICHARD, CAPT.
North Carolina, Oregon DAR Daughter

W

WAGENSAILER, JOHN, PVT.
Pennsylvania, Oregon DAR Daughter

WAINSCOTT, ABRAHAM
North Carolina DAR Daughter Sandra Fuller

WALDEN, RICHARD, SR.
Virginia, Oregon DAR Daughter

WALDRON, PETER
New York, Oregon DAR Daughter

WALKER, JOHN, SR.
New Hampshire, DAR Daughter Sandra Fuller

WALKER, JOHN, SGT.
Massachusetts, Oregon DAR Daughter

WALLACE, JOSIAH
Massachusetts, Oregon DAR Daughter

WALLER, BENJAMIN
Virginia, Oregon DAR Daughter

WALTMAN, CONRAD, JR.
Pennsylvania, Oregon DAR Daughter

WAMPLER, GEORGE, SR.
Pennsylvania, Oregon DAR Daughter

WARD, JOHN, PVT.
Connecticut, Oregon DAR Daughter

WARE, WILLIAM, PVT.
North Carolina, Oregon DAR Daughter

WARLICK, BARBARA
North Carolina, Oregon DAR Daughter

WARNER, ELIPHAZ
Vermont, Oregon DAR Daughter

WARNER, NATHAN, CPL.
Massachusetts, Oregon DAR Daughter

WARNER, WILLIAM
Connecticut, Oregon DAR Daughter

WARREN, CALEB DENNIS
Vermont, Oregon DAR Daughter

WARREN, GIDEON
New Hampshire, Oregon DAR Daughter

WARREN, MARTIN, PVT.
Virginia, Oregon DAR Daughter

WALLS, GEORGE
SAR Compatriot Joseph Williams

WARD, DAVID
Connecticut, Oregon DAR Daughter

WARE, SAMUEL
SAR Compatriot Donald Wear

WARNER, JONATHAN, LT.
Massachusetts, Oregon DAR Daughter

WARNER, NATHANIEL
Connecticut, Oregon DAR Daughter

WASHBURN, JOSEPH
SAR Compatriot Donald Sass

WASHBURN, JOSEPH, PVT.
New York, Oregon DAR Daughter

WASHINGTON, JOHN AUGUSTINE
Virginia, Oregon DAR Daughter

WATERMAN, DANIEL, SR., PVT.
Vermont, Oregon DAR Daughter

WATKINS, EVAN
Virginia, Oregon DAR Daughter

WATKINS, NATHAN, CAPT.
Massachusetts, Oregon DAR Daughter

WATTS, NICHOLAS
Massachusetts, Oregon DAR Daughter

WAUGH, JOHN, PVT.
Pennsylvania, Oregon DAR Daughter

WEAVER, SAMUEL J.
Virginia, Oregon DAR Daughter

WEAVER, SAMUEL
North Carolina, Oregon DAR Daughter

WEBBER, BRADLEY
Massachusetts, Oregon DAR Daughter

WEBSTER, CONSTANT, SR.
Massachusetts, Oregon DAR Daughter

WEBSTER, JONATHAN
Connecticut, Oregon DAR Daughter

WEED, ELEAZER, PVT.
Connecticut, Oregon DAR Daughter

WEED, GILBERT, PVT.
Connecticut, Oregon DAR Daughter

WEED, JOHN, JR.
Connecticut, Oregon DAR Daughter

WEEKS, PHILLIP, PVT.
Connecticut, Oregon DAR Daughter

WEIDNER, HEINRICH
North Carolina, Oregon DAR Daughter

WELLS, JOSEPH, MAJ.
New York, Oregon DAR Daughter

WELLS, SHAYLOR, PVT.
New York, Oregon DAR Daughter

WENTZ, JOHAN JOST
Pennsylvania, Oregon DAR Daughter

WEST, THOMAS
Virginia, Oregon DAR Daughter

WETZEL, ADAMA
Virginia, Oregon DAR Daughter

WHALEY, JAMES, JR., 2ND LT.
Virginia, Oregon DAR Daughter

WHALEY, JAMES, SR.
Virginia, Oregon DAR Daughter

WHEALDON, ISAAC
SAR Compatriot John Krumbein

WHEAT, THOMAS
New Hampshire, Oregon DAR Daughter

WHEELER, AARON, SR.
Oregon DAR Daughter

WHEELER, PETER, PVT.
New Hampshire, DAR Daughter Janice Gadway Gardner

WHICKER, JAMES
North Carolina, Oregon DAR Daughter

WHITAKER, JOSEPH
Pennsylvania, Oregon DAR Daughter

WHITAKER, JOSHUA
SAR Compatriot George Lanning

WHITE, JOHN, PVT.
New York, DAR Daughter Evelyn Laughman,

WHITE, JOHN, PVT.
Connecticut, Oregon DAR Daughter

WHITE, JOSEPH, PVT.
Virginia, Oregon DAR Daughter

WHITE, THOMAS
SAR Compatriot Thompson White

WHITE, THOMAS
Pennsylvania, Oregon DAR Daughter

WHITE, WILLIAM
Maryland, Oregon DAR Daughter

WHITENER, HENRY, JR.
North Carolina, Oregon DAR Daughter

WHITMARSH, JACOB
Massachusetts, Oregon DAR Daughter

WHITNER, HENRY. JR.
North Carolina, Oregon DAR Daughter

WHITNEY, JOSHUA, SGT.
Massachusetts, Oregon DAR Daughter

WHITNEY, WILLIAM, PVT.
New York, Oregon DAR Daughter

WHITSITT, WILLIAM WIRT WHITESIDE
Pennsylvania, Oregon DAR Daughter

WHITTIER, DANIEL
New Hampshire, SAR Compatriot Robert Whittier, Oregon DAR Daughter

WHITTINGTON, ISSAC
Maryland, Oregon DAR Daughter

WHITTLESEY, ELIPHALET, JR., PVT.
Massachusetts, Oregon DAR Daughter

WICKER, ROBERT
South Carolina, Oregon DAR Daughter

WICKIZER, CONRAD
   Pennsylvania, Oregon DAR Daughter

WILDER, THOMAS
   Connecticut, Oregon DAR Daughter

WILHOIT, JESSE
   Virginia, Oregon DAR Daughter

WILKINS, JAMES
   DAR Daughter Belle Passi Chapter

WILLETT, GEORGE
   Virginia, Oregon DAR Daughter

WILLETT, GRACE
   Maryland, Oregon DAR Daughter

WILLEY, ABSALOM
   DAR Daughter Belle Passi Chapter

WILLIAM, PORTER, LTCOL.
   Rutherford Militia 1776-1782 SAR Compatriot Eric Salbeda

WILLIAMS, BENJAMIN
   Pennsylvania, Oregon DAR Daughter

WILLIAMS, DANIEL, CAPT.
   Oregon DAR Daughter

WILLIAMS, HARDIN
   SAR Compatriot Bennett Wight

WILLIAMS, ISRAEL
   Connecticut, Oregon DAR Daughter

WILLIAMS, JAMES
   South Carolina, Georgia, Oregon DAR Daughter

WILLIAMS, JOHN
   Virginia, DAR Daughter Belle Passi Chapter

WILLIS, STOUGHTON
   Massachusetts, Oregon DAR Daughter

WILLSON, NAHUM
Massachusetts, Oregon DAR Daughter

WILSON, ANDREW, PVT.
Virginia, Oregon DAR Daughter

WILSON, JAMES
Pennsylvania, SAR Compatriot Christopher Bullard, Oregon DAR Daughter

WILSON, JESSIE
New Hampshire, Oregon DAR Daughter

WILSON, MATTHEW, PVT.
Pennsylvania, Oregon DAR Daughter

WILSON, ROBERT
DAR Daughter Patti Waitman-Ingebretsen

WILSON, WILLIAM, PVT.
Pennsylvania, Oregon DAR Daughter

WINANS, LEWIS
New Jersey, Oregon DAR Daughter

WINCKELBLECK, JOHN ADAM
Pennsylvania, Oregon DAR Daughter

WINSLOW, EZRA
Massachusetts, Oregon DAR Daughter

WITHERSPOON, JOHN
Signer of Declaration of Independence SAR Compatriots Johnny Alexander, Tyler McClintock

WITT, ELISHA, PVT.
Virginia, Oregon DAR Daughter

WIXOM, JOHN
New York, Oregon DAR Daughter

WIXOM, PELEG
New York, Oregon DAR Daughter

WOLCOTT, GIDEON, SGT.
New York, Oregon DAR Daughter

WOMACK, ABRAHAM
Georgia, Oregon DAR Daughter

WOOD, JEREMIAH, PVT.
New Jersey, Oregon DAR Daughter

WOODMANSEE, JAMES, LT.
New Jersey, Oregon DAR Daughter

WOODS, ABIJA
Kentucky, Oregon DAR Daughter

WOODS, ADAM, SGT.
Virginia, Oregon DAR Daughter

WOODS, HUGH
DAR Daughter Patti Waitman-Ingebretsen

WOODS, JOHN
DAR Daughter Patti Waitman-Ingebretsen

WOODS, SAMUEL, PVT.
Indian Scout Cumberland Co. Pennsylvania Militia SAR Compatriots Johnny Alexander, Tyler McClintock

WOODS, SOLOMON, LT.
Massachusetts, Oregon DAR Daughter

WOODS, SUSANNAH WALLACE
Virginia, Oregon DAR Daughter

WOODWORTH, GERSHOM
New York, Oregon DAR Daughter

WOOLDRIDGE, RICHARD
Virginia, Oregon DAR Daughter

WOOLVERTON, DANIEL
New Jersey, Oregon DAR Daughte

WORD, CHARLES, NONCOM.
Virginia, Oregon DAR Daughter

WORDEN, JOSEPH
SAR Compatriots Steven Boedigheimer, Michael Boedigheimer

WORDEN, NATHANIEL
New York, Oregon DAR Daughter

WORKMAN, JACOB, PVT.
Maryland, Oregon DAR Daughter

WRIGHT, BENJAMIN
North Carolina, Oregon DAR Daughter

WRIGHT, ELISHA, CPL.
Massachusetts, Oregon DAR Daughter

WRIGHT, ISAAC
South Carolina, DAR Daughter Belle Passi Chapter

WRIGHT, ITHAMAR
SAR Compatriot David Kingsella

WRIGHT, RICHARD, SR.
North Carolina, Oregon DAR Daughter

WRIGHT, ROBERT
Virginia, Oregon DAR Daughter

WRIGHT, STEPHEN, PVT.
Drummer in Capt. Wright's Co. battle of White Plains, 28 Oct 17761776 - 1780 SAR Compatriot Steven Waters
Born 24, May 1764 Died 16, Feb 1857.
The following was cut and pasted from the book "Soldiers and Sailors of the Revolutionary War".
Wright, Stephen, Westford. Drummer, Capt. Zaccheus Wright's Co., Col. Brooks' regt.; return dated Camp at White Plains, Oct. 31, 1776; reported as in camp and fit for duty; also, Capt. Joshua Parker's co.. Col. Robinson's Regt.; enlisted Sept. 15, 1777; service to Jan.1, 1778, at Rhode Island; also Private, Capt. John Porter's co.. Col. Cyprian How's regt. Col. Commandant John Jacobs's brigade; entered service July 25, 1780; discharged Oct. 30, 1780; Service, 3 MOS. 10 days, at Rhode Island, including travel (80 miles) home. Regiment raised for 3 months.

WYATT, JOSHUA
Massachusetts, Oregon DAR Daughter

Y

YANDLE, JAMES
North Carolina, Oregon DAR Daughter

YAPLE, JACOB, PVT.
Col. Wynkoop's Reg. New York SAR Compatriot Arlen Clark

YAPLE, PHILLIP H.
Patriot New York SAR Compatriot Arlen Clark

YEAGER, ADAM, SR.
Virginia, Oregon DAR Daughter

YEAGER, JOHN
Virginia, Oregon DAR Daughter

YEASLEY, GEORGE
DAR Daughter Belle Passi Chapter

YERKES, JAMES, PVT.
New York, Oregon DAR Daughter

YOUNG, ELKANAH
Massachusetts, Oregon DAR Daughter

YOUNG, JACOB
North Carolina, SAR Compatriots Charles Thomas, Patrick Thomas

YOUNG, JOHN, PVT.
Massachusetts, Oregon DAR Daughter

Z

ZACHARY, JAMES, PVT.
Georgia, Oregon DAR Daughter

ZEHNER, ADAM
Pennsylvania, Oregon DAR Daughter

ZIMMERMAN, GEORGE
Maryland, Oregon DAR Daughter

ZUMWALT, ADAM
Virginia, Oregon DAR Daughter

ZUMWALT, CHRISTOPHER
Virginia, Oregon DAR Daughter

ZUMWALT, JACOB
Virginia, Oregon DAR Daughter

Name Index

A

Abbott, Joseph   18
Abbott, William   18
Adams, Gilbert   18
Adams, Joel   18
Adams, John   18
Adams, Mathew   18
Adams, Oliver   18
Adams, Samuel   18
Adsit, Benjamin   18
Akers, Thomas   55, 107
Albright, Bernard, Pvt.   18
Alden, Silas, Lt.   18
Alexander, James   18, 19
Alexander, Johnny   25, 55, 82, 88, 125, 133, 134
Alexander, William, Lt.   18
Alger, Kenneth   78
Allen, Ananias   19
Allen, Isham, Pvt.   19
Allen, Janis   101
Allen, Job, Capt.   19
Allen, John, Pvt.   19
Allen, Malcum   19
Allis, Moses, Sgt.   19
Alspach, Henry   19
Alston, Joseph John   19
Alston, Willis Wilson, Col.   19
Alstott, John   19
Altman, John Peter   19
Ammidown, Philip   19
Anderson, Absolom   19
Anderson, Benjamin   19
Anderson, Elijah   19
Anderson, Joseph   20
Anderson, William Clark   20
Andrews, Robert   20
Andrews, William   20
Antes, John Henry, Sr.   20
Appleby, James   20
Applegate, Daniel   20
App, Michael, Pvt.   20
Arendall, Nathan   20

Armstrong, Joshua, Pvt.   20
Arsenault. Brayden   60
Arthur, John   20
Ashcraft, Ichabod   20
Ashley, William, Sgt.   20
Ashmead, John   20
Atkinson, John, Pvt.   20
Atwood, Elisha   21
Atwood, Zaccheus   21
Austin, David, Pvt.   21
Austin, Silas   21
Austin Sr, David   21

B

Babcock, Rueben, Pvt.   21
Bager, John George, Rev.   21
Bagley, Harmon   21
Bailey, Richard   21
Bailey, Richard, Sr.   21
Bailey, Samuel   21
Bailey Sr, Richard   21
Baker, Benajah, Pvt.   32
Baker, David   22
Baker, Joseph   22
Baker Jr, Moses   22
Baker, Moses, Jr.   22
Baker, Samuel   22
Balch, Benjamin   22
Baldwin, Thomas   22
Ballenger, James   22
Ball, William, Lt.   22
Banks, James   22
Banks, Joshua   22
Banks, Thomas   22
Banner, Casper   22
Barker, Jeff   108
Barkley, Jacob   21
Barnes, Keith   37
Barnes, Wyatt   37
Barnett, Philip   22
Barnett, Robert   23
Barnum, Abijah   23
Barrett, Jonathan, Pvt.   23

Bartlet, Josiah, Col.   23
Bartlett, Susannah Davis   23
Bartlett, Thomas   23
Barton, Elisha   23
Barwick, William   23
Basham, Obediah, Pvt.   23
Bassett, Jotham   23
Bassett, Rufus   23
Batcheller/Batchelder,
   Benjamin   23
Bathhurst, Lawrence   23
Baxter, Pettie   23
Bayard, Stephen   23
Beal, Joseph   24
Beal, Joshua, Pvt   24
Bealle Sr, Benjamin   24
Beaman, Elijah, Lt.   24
Beam, Henry   24
Bean, William   24
Beatty, John   24
Beckett, Humphrey   24
Bedient, Mordecai, Pvt.   24
Bedinger, Peter   24
Beer, Robert   24
Beers, Joel, Pvt.   24
Belew, Solomon, Pvt.   24
Belle Passi Chapter   22, 25, 26,
   30, 31, 32, 34, 36, 37, 40,
   41, 42, 46, 47, 49, 54, 59,
   60, 62, 65, 66, 68, 69, 71,
   72, 74, 75, 76, 78, 81, 82,
   84, 85, 86, 87, 88, 90, 93,
   94, 98, 99, 101, 103, 105,
   108, 109, 112, 114, 115,
   121, 123, 124, 126, 132,
   135, 136
Bellows, Thomas   25
Bell, Robert   24
Bell, Thomas, Pvt.   24
Benedict, Samuel, Pvt.   25
Bennett, Batchelor, Cpl.   25
Bennett, Isaac   25
Bennett Jr., Joshua   25

Benson, Peter, Pvt.   25
Benson, Stephen, Cpl.   25
Bent, David   25
Bertram, William   25
Bess, Peter   25
Betterton, Ken   20
Betty, George   25
Bible, John Adam   25
Bickel, Peter   25
Bicknell, John   25
Biery, Henry   25
Biery, Michael, NonCom.   26
Biggs, Robert   25
Billings, Thaddeus   26
Bingham, Jonathon   26
Bishop, William, Pvt.   26
Blackburn, Thomas   26
Blair, Brice   26
Blanchard, Daniel   26
Blanchard, Daniel, Sr., Pvt   26
Bland, Thomas   26
Blare, James   26
Blasdel, Jacob   26
Bliss, James   26
Bliss, Nathan, Pvt.   26
Blood, Simon   26
Bloomer, Reuben, Ens.   27
Blount, Walter   27
Blue, John Jr, Pvt.   27
Boardman, Edward   40, 54, 82
Boardman, Tom   40, 54, 82, 92
Boatwright, James   27
Bockoven, George, Lt.   27
Boedigheimer, Michael   135
Boedigheimer, Steven   135
Bogardus, Bradley   65
Bogardus, Brian   65
Bogardus, John   65
Bogardus, Robert   69, 84
Bolling (Bowling), Jarrett,
   Pvt.   27
Bomberger, John, Pvt.   25
Bonnell, Jerry   83

Boone, Edward   27
Boone, Rebecca Bryan   29
Boone, Squire, Sgt.   29
Boone Sr, Josiah   29
Boring, Dean   60
Bostwich, Benjamin   29
Bosworth, Constant   29
Bosworth, Nathaniel, Cpl.   30
Botts, John   30
Bourne Sr, Stephen   30
Bowen, Henry   30
Bowen, Lily McIlhaney   30
Bowlsby, Daniel   30
Bowlsby, Samuel, Pvt.   30
Bowman, Philip   29, 30
Bowser, John   30
Boyden, John   30
Boyd, James   30
Boyer, Casper   30
Boynton, Amos   30
Bozarth, Joseph   30
Bracken, Isaac   25
Bradbury, Benjamin, Sgt.   31
Bradish, Daniel   31
Bradley, Elisha   31
Branch, Edward   31
Breed, Oliver   31
Brenton, James   31
Bricker, John, Jr., Cpl.   31
Bridgforth, Benjamin   31
Bridgforth, James   31
Bridgham Sr, John   31
Briggs, Owen   31
Brigham, Asa, Maj.   31
Briscoe, Henry, Pvt.   31
Britton, Pendleton, Pvt.   31
Broaddus, Thomas   31
Brock, Jesse   32
Brockway, Ebenezer   32
Brokaw, Isaac   31
Brookhart/Burkheart, Philip   29
Brookhart, Kenneth   32
Brooks, William   32

Brough, Hermanus, Sr.   32
Brown, Amos, Sgt.   32
Brown, Ephraim   32
Brown, Hezekiah   32
Brown, Joseph   32
Brown, Knight   32
Brown, Lewis   32
Brown, Rufus   32
Brown, Samuel   32
Brown, Thomas   32
Bruce, John, Sgt.   33
Buchanan, George   33
Buchanan, Robert, Capt.   33
Bucklin, John   33
Buckner, William   33
Buell, Jr., Jedediah   33
Bull, Ambrose   32
Bullard, Christopher   133
Burcham SR, John   33
Burkhalter, John Peter, Jr., Ens.   33
Burkhalter, Peter, Sr., LtCol.   33
Burkhart, George   33
Burnham, Ammi   33
Burns, William, Pvt.   33
Bush, James   33
Bushnell, Gideon   33
Bushnell, John Handley   34
Butcher, Fred   89, 120
Butcher, Samuel   33
Butler, Joseph   34
Butts, Sherabiah, Cpt.   34
Butz, John   34
Buzbee, Jacob   34
Byam, Samuel, Pvt.   32

C

Cable, Abraham   34
Cady, Stodard   34
Cain, Daniel   34
Caldwell, Robert   34
Calhoun, Rebecca Floride Pickens   34

Calkins, John 34
Callaway Sr, Thomas 34
Callender, John, Lt. 35
Campbell, Archibald 35
Campbell, Charles, Pvt. 35
Campbell, James 35
Campbell, McDonald 35
Campbell, William, Corp. 35
Campfield, William 35
Camp, Job 35
Canfield, Daniel 35
Cannon, James 35
Cannon, Samuel 35
Carder, Albert 42
Carpenter, Adam, Pvt. 35
Carpenter, Ann Shutley 35
Carpenter, Daniel 36
Carpenter, George, Sr., Pvt. 35
Carpenter, John, Pvt. 36
Carr, Gideon 36
Carr, John 36
Carr, John Fendell 36
Carroll, William 34
Carter, George 36
Carter, John B. 36
Carter, Levi 36
Carter, Peter 36
Carter, Samuel 36
Cartwright, Peter 36
Castor, Frederick, Lt. 36
Cave, Richard, Rev. 36
Chaffee, Ezra, Capt. 36
Chaffin, Ephraim, Pvt. 37
Chain, William 37
Chalfant, Solomon, Pvt. 37
Chambers, Matthew 37
Champlin, Charles 37
Chandler, William, Pvt. 37
Chapin, Phineas 37
Chapman, James 37
Chapman, John 37
Chase, Berry, Sgt. 37
Chase, Caleb 34

Cheesebrough, Perez, Pvt. 37
Cheeseman, Richard 37
Chenoweth, Thomas 37
Cherry, Joshua 38
Childs Jr., Daniel 38
Chiles, William 38
Christian, Phillip, Pvt. 38
Church, Giles 37
Clapp, Samuel 38
Clark, Arlen 24, 27, 47, 49, 54, 58, 77, 108, 111, 115, 126, 136
Clark, Benjamin 38
Clarke, Elisha, Pvt. 38
Clark, Elton 62
Clark, Hezekiah, Pvt. 38
Clark, James, Pvt. 38
Clark, John 38
Clark, Jonas 40
Clark, Matthew 38
Claxton, Aaron 103
Claxton, Jeffrey 103
Claxton, Stefan 103
Claypoole, Sr., John 38
Clem, Michael 38
Clendenin, John 39
Cleveland, Isaac 39
Cleveland, Josiah 39
Cleveland, Larkin, Capt. 39
Cleveland, William, Sr., Pvt. 39
Clifton, Nathan 39
Cluggage, Gaven, Cpt. 39
Clute, John 39
Cochran, James 39
Cockrum, Benjamin 39
Coddington, Benjamin 39
Coe, Joel 39
Coffeen, Henry 39
Coffin, William 39
Colburn, Benjamin, Pvt. 39
Colburn, Robert, Sr. 40
Colclough, William 40
Cole, Abiel 40

Cole, James, Lt.   40
Cole, Joseph   40
Coleman, Jacob   40
Coleman, John   40
Collier, John   40
Colton, Ebenezer   40
Combs, John, Sr.   40
Combs Sr., John   40
Comegys, Abraham, Sr.   40
Comegys Sr., Abraham,   40
Comstock, Abel   40
Comstock, Medad   40
Condit, Jabez   40
Condit, Philip   40
Cone, Joshua   41
Cone, William   41
Conger, David   41
Cooke, Elisha   41
Cook, Eli   41
Coombs, John, Sr.   41
Coombs, Mason, Sr.   41
Coons, Jacob Jr.   41
Cooper, Thomas, Pvt.   41
Copeland, Dennis   41
Corn, John Peter   41
Cornwell, William   40, 41
Correll, John   41
Corwin, Richard   41
Cotton, Samuel J.   41
Cottrell, Asa   42
Couch, Benjamin, Pvt.   42
Coulter, Robert   42
Countryman, Conrad   42
Covalt, Abraham, Capt.   42
Covell, Ezra   42
Covey, Walter   42
Covington, Francis S.   41
Cowan, Ernest   64
Cox, Phineas   36
Coy, John   42
Coyner, Casper   42
Craig, David   42
Craig, Mary Polly Hawkins   42

Crapo, Peter, Pvt.   42
Crary, Nathan, Pvt.   43
Craven, Thomas   43
Crawford, David   43
Crawford, James   42
Crawford, Joel   43
Craw, Reuben, Pvt.   43
Creswell Jr., Robert   43
Creswell, Robert, Jr.   43
Creswell, Thomas   43
Creswell, William   43
Crigler, Christopher   43
Croninger, Leonard , Pvt.   43
Crosby.., Hannah   43
Crosby, Stephen   43
Crosby, Thomas, Pvt.   43
Crowell, Henry   43
Crow, Jacob, Pvt.   43
Crum, Richard, Pvt.   43
Crutchlow, James, Pvt.   44
Culbertson, Robert   44
Culver, David, Pvt.   44
Culver, Nathaniel   44
Cummings, Noble   44
Cunliffe, Stephen   123
Currier, Moses   44
Curry, James, Capt.   44
Cutler, Joseph   44

D

Daggett, John   44
Dale, George   44
Dalton, David   44
Dalton, John   44
Dalton, Samuel, Sr.   44
Dalton Sr., Samuel   44
Danforth, David   44, 45
Danforth, Enoch   45
Daron, Adam, Pvt.   45
Davidson, John   45
Davidson, William   45
Davis, Caleb   45
Davis, Edward   45

Davis, James, Pvt.   45
Davis, John   45
Davis, Paul   45
Davis, Samson, Sgt.   45
Davis Sr., Issac   45
Davis Sr, William, Capt.   45
Davis, William , Jr., Pvt.   45
Day, Abraham   45
Day, Ezera   45
Dean, Benjamin, Pvt.   46
Dean, Enos, Sgt.   46
Dean, Jedediah   44
Deeds, John   46
Degner, George   22
De Hart, Hendrick   46
Delano, Thomas, Jr Sgt Maj   46
De la Roche, Frederick
    Franck   46
De Merit, John II, Maj.   46
Denney, Patrick   46
Dennison, David   46
De Noriega, Jose Vincente
    Garcia   46
Dent, John   46
Denton, Solomon   46
Deschler, Adam   46
Deupree (Dupree), Joseph   46
Devin, David   47
Devin, Gary   47
Devin Jr., William   46
Devin, Michael   47
Devin, Steven   47
DeWeese, Samuel   47
Dewey, Stephen   47
Dewey, William, Cpl.   47
Dewing, Jabez   47
Deyo, Peter, Pvt.   47
Dial, Joseph   47
Dicks, James   47
Dicks, Peter   44
Diefenbaugh, Michael, Lt.   47
Dillard, William, Pvt.   47
Dilley, Revidel, Pvt.   47
Dimmick, Eliphant   47

Dimmick, Solomon, Lt.   47
Ditto, Francis L., Pvt.   47
Dix, Elijah   48
Dixwell, Lothrop, Pvt.   48
Doak, Sr., David   48
Dodson, George   48
Dolson, John, Sgt.   48
Donaldson, Isaac, Pvt.   48
Dorrance, Samuel, Pvt.   48
Dorsey, Daniel, Capt.   48
Doty, Phillip, Sgt.   48
Doty, William   48
Douse, Joseph, Sgt.   48
Dowler, Edward   48
Downey, Darb, Capt.   48
Doyle, Barnabas, Pvt.   48
Drake, George   48
Drake, Thomas   49
Draper, John   49
Dudley, Asa, Pvt.   49
Dudley, Samuel, Staff Officer   49
Duer, John   49
Duer, Richard   49
Dumont, Peter, Sgt.   49
Dunbar, Thomas   49
Duncan, Elizabeth
    Alexander   49
Duncan, Moses   49
Duncan Sr, William   49
Duncan, William, Sr.   49
Dunham, John, Pvt.   49
Dunlap, Samuel, Pvt.   49
Dunnington Jr., William   49
Dunnington Sr., William   49
Durfee, Gideon, Pvt.   49
Durkee, Benjamin   50
Dutcher, Cornelius   50
Dye, Andrew   50
Dyer Jr., Henry   50
Dysart, John, Sgt.   50

E

Eager, William   50

Eaton, William   50
Ebaugh, John   50
Eck, Theodorus, Pvt.   50
Eddy, Abel   50
Eddy, Zachariah   50
Edgington, Joseph   50
Edwards, David   50
Edwards, John, Sr.   50
Elder, Robert   51
Eldrege (Eldridge), Phineas   51
Elkins, Robert   51
Elston, David   51
Emerson, Jonathan   51
Emery, Ambrose, Pvt.   51
Engle. Phillip   51
Erwin, Arthur, Col.   51
Erwin, Francis   52
Erwin, Jackson   51, 95
Erwin, Phillip   51
Erwin, Riley   94
Eskridge, Burdett   52
Eskridge, Thomas   46
Esselstyne, Conradt   52
Estabrook, Ebenezer   52
Eubank, John   52
Evans, John   52
Everett Sr., Ebenezer   52
Ewer, John   52
Ewing, William, Pvt.   52
Ezell, John   52

F

Fairbanks, John, Lt.   52
Fairfield, William   53
Fannin, Laughlin   53
Farley, Daniel, Pvt.   53
Farmer, James   53
Farmum, Levi   53
Farrington, Frederick, Pvt.   53
Farr, Thomas   53
Faucett, William   53
Faust, Adam   53
Fearing, Abel   53

Fearing, James   53
Felton, Benjamin, Lt. Adj.   53
Fenton, Samuel, Capt.   53
Ferguson, David   53
Ferguson, John   53
Field, John Van Wyck   54
Finley, James   54
Fisher, Jacob   54
Fisk, William   54
Fitch, Timothy   54
Flagg, Peter   54
Fleming, Elijah   54
Fleming, Robert, Sr.   54
Fletcher, Benjamin   54
Flint, William   54
Flood, Daniel, Pvt.   54
Flora, Joseph J., Sr.   54
Fogelsanger, Jacob   54
Folsom, Daniel   54
Foote, Henry   53
Ford, Jacob, Sr.   55
Fore, Peter   55
Forqueran, John   55
Forqueran, Peter, Sr.   55
Fortson, Thomas   55
Foster, Ezekiel   55
Foster, Hezekiah, Pvt.   55
Foster, Richard   55
Foster, Richard, Sr.   55
Fowler, Godfrey   55
Fowler, Joshua, Cpl.   55
Francisco, Ludwick   55
Freedland, Thomas   82
French, Seba, Cpl.   55
Frink, Isaac   55
Frink, Ruth Pinckney   56
Frisbie, Philemon   56
Frost, Samuel   56
Fruge, Pierre Antoine   56
Frutchey, Frederick   56
Fuller, Abraham   56
Fuller, Sandra   127
Fullerton, Alexander   56

Fultz, Gordon 20
Fuson, William 56
Futrell, Thomas 56

G

Gadway Gardner, Janice 34, 39, 40, 88, 120, 130
Gaines, Ambrose 56
Gaines, Thomas, Cpl. 56
Gambil, Martin 56
Gano, James 56
Gard, Daniel 56
Gardner, John 57
Gardner, Joseph 57
Gardner, Martin 57
Gardner, William 57
Garnett, Anthony, Cpl. 57
Garnett, Reuben 57
Garrett, Ambrose 57
Garrett, Francis, Jr., Pvt. 57
Garrison, James 57
Garvin, Thomas, Pvt. 57
Garvin, Thomas, Sgt. 57
Gass Sr., David 57
Gates, Jonathan, Pvt. 57
Gates, Silas, Pvt. 57
Gault, Matthew 57
Gaylord, Aaron, Lt. 58
Gentry, Benejah 58
Genung, Thomas 58
Gerard, John 58
Gibbs, Hezekiah 58
Giffin, Edward 58
Giffin, John 58
Giffin, Simon 58
Gift, Johan A., Pvt. 59
Gilbert, Gardner 58
Gilbert, Joseph, Sgt. 58
Gilham, Peter 58
Gillam, Jonathan, Pvt. 58
Gillespie, Daniel, Capt. 58
Gillette, Joseph 58
Gilliam, Hinchea 59
Gilliam, James 59
Gillihan, William, Pvt. 59
Gilstrap, Peter 59
Gish, George 59
Gish, John G 59
Gish Sr., Christian 59
Glantz, Johannes, Pvt. 59
Glass, Johann Mathias 59
Glazier, John, Pvt. 59
Glen, Jacob 115
Glen, John 115
Glen, Mason 115
Glenn, Sue 24, 26, 32, 34, 41, 44, 78, 116, 117
Glidden, Benjamin 59
Goble, Stephen 59
Goff Sr, John 59
Goin, Thomas 59
Goldsmith, John, Sr 59
Goode, Samuel 60
Goodrich, Elnathan 60
Goodrich, James 60
Goodrich, Thomas, Pvt. 60
Goodrich, Waitstill 60
Goodson, William, Ens. 60
Gordon, Jesse 59
Gormley, Hugh 60
Goss, Elizabeth X 60
Gott, Story 60
Gould, Solomon 60
Gourley, Hugh 60
Graham, Peter, Pvt. 60
Grammer, Joseph, Pvt. 60
Grant, Benjamin, Pvt. 61
Grant Sr., William 61
Graves, Ann 62
Graves, David 62
Graves, John 62
Greely, Shubal 62
Greenlee, William 62
Greenwood, Bartlee 62
Gregg, Israel, Pvt. 62
Gregg, Robert 62

Gregory, Uriah 62
Grier, Henry, Lt. 56
Grier, Henry, Lt., 56
Grier, John 62
Grier, Thomas 62
Griffin, Sherrod, Sgt. 62
Griswold, John, Pvt. 63
Guiel, William 68
Guillion, Jeremiah, Pvt. 63
Gunnison Sr, Samuel, Cpt. 63
Guthrey, Henry 63

H

Hadley, Simon 63
Haggard, Nathaniel 63
Hale, Isaac 63
Hale, Reuben 63
Halferty, Edward, Pvt. 63
Hall, Caleb 63
Hall, David 63
Hall, Edward, Pvt. 63
Halley, Francis 64
Halley, James, Sr. 64
Hall, George Abbott 64
Hall, James 63
Hall, Lawrence Rubin 64
Hall, Leonard 64
Halsey, John, Pvt. 64
Halsey, Sylvanus 64
Hamar, James, Pvt. 64
Hamilton, Silas 64
Handy, Samuel 64
Haney, John 64
Haney, Robert 64
Hanlin, Patrick 64
Hapgood Jr, Asa, Pvt. 64
Harbaugh, Yost 64
Harbour, Joel, Pvt. 64
Hardaway, John, Lt. 64
Hardaway, Thomas 65
Harding, Henry, Sr. 65
Harding, Ian 65
Harding, Kevin 65

Harding, Stephen 64, 65
Harding, Wilmoth George 65
Hardy, Ephraim 65
Harker, Daniel 65
Harker, Joseph 65
Harlow, Zacheus 65
Harmon, John 65
Harmon, Thomas 65
Harper, Richard, Pvt. 65
Harrave, John, Sr Pvt. 65
Harrington, Henry 65
Harrington, Sampson 65
Harrington, Thomas 65
Harris, Henry 66
Harris, Nicholas 66
Harrison, James Mason 66
Harshman, Peter 66
Hart, Timothy, Sgt. 66
Harvey, Thomas, Pvt. 66
Harvey, William, Pvt. 66
Harvey, Zephoniah 65
Haskell, Josiah, Pvt. 66
Haskell, William 66
Haskins, Ebenezer, Sgt. 66
Hassan, Hugh 66
Hatch, Jethro 66
Hatch, Joseph 66
Hawes, Ichabod, Pvt. 66
Hawkins, Amaziah 67
Hawkins, Uriah 67
Hawks, Abjah 67
Haycraft, Samuel 67
Haynes, Jonathon 67
Haynes, Thomas 67
Haynie, William, 2nd Lt. 67
Head, Benjamin, Cpt. 67
Head, James, Ens. 67
Heald, Benjamin, Pvt. 67
Heald, Ephraim 67
Heard, Thomas 67
Heath, Joseph Jr., 67
Heath, Joshua 67
Heckethorne, Larry 64

Heiserman, Fred 79
Helfferich, John, Jr., Pvt. 67
Henderson, Pleasant, Maj. 68
Hendren/Hendron, John 68
Henning, Christophel 68
Henry, Robert 123
Herrick, Amos 68
Herrick, Henry, Sgt. 68
Hesley, Lenard, Pvt. 68
Hester, Abraham 68
Hewitt, Nicholas 68
Hichborn, Robert, Lt. 68
Higley, Joel, 2nd Lt. 63
Higley, Seth 69
Hiller, Martin Pvt. 69
Hilley, Thomas 69
Hilliard, Daniel, SMN 69
Hill, John 69
Hill, Thomas 69
Hiltz, Godfrey/Gotfried 69
Hinch, Samuel 69
Hinkle, John Justus 69
Hisey, John 69
Hitchcock, Phineas, Sr., Pvt. 69
Hitt, Peter 69
Hixon/Hickson, John 69
Hoblit, Johannes 69
Hockenberry, Casper 69
Hockenberry, Peter 70
Hodge, Charles 70
Hogg, James 70
Holbrook, Silas 70
Holland, Thomas 70
Holleman, Jesse 70
Hollis, Elijah 70
Holloway, Elkanah 70
Holloway, Thomas 70
Holman, Elisha, Sgt. 70
Holmes, James 70
Holmes, Lemuel, Capt. 70
Hooper, Absalom 70
Hoopes, Ezra 70
Hoover, Henry 70

Hortenstine, John 71
Horton, Nathaniel, Pvt. 71
Hotchkiss, Daniel, Pvt. 71
Hotchkiss, Mark 71
Hottenstein, Jacob 69
Houston, James 71
Houtz, Jacob 71
Hovey, Samuel 71
Howard, Peter 71
Howes, Jeremiah 71
Howland, Caleb 71
Howland Jr., Jon 71
Hoyt, Jonathan 71
Hoyt, Thomas 71
Hudson, David 71
Hudson, William 72
Hughes, Jonathan 69
Hughey, James, Sgt. 72
Hume, George 72
Humphrey, Elisha 72
Hunter, David 72
Hunter, Henry, Pvt. 72
Hurst, Henry 72
Hush, Valentine 72
Hutchinson, Cornelius 72
Hutchinson, James, Pvt. 71

I

Ingalls, Israel, Sgt. 72
Ingebretsen. Grier 3, 13, 62
Ingham, Alexander, Pvt. 72
Ingraham , Duncan 72
Irwin, John 72
Isbell, Fred 42
Ives, Nathaniel, Jr., Pvt. 73
Ives, Nathaniel, Sr. 73

J

Jack Pinney 100
James, Arron 73
Jan Dial 47
Jenkins Jr., John 73
Jenkins Sr., John 73

Jewett Sr, Moses, Capt.   73
Johnson, Griffith, Capt.   73
Johnson, Moses   73
Johnson, Robert   73
Johnston, Zachariah, Capt.   73
Jones, Jacob   73
Jones, John   73
Jones, Russell   73
Jones Sr., Adam Crane, Capt.   73
Jones, Thomas, Maj.   74
Jordan, William   74
Joseph, Daniel   74
Joslin, Hezekiah   74
Joyner, Thomas   74
Junkin, Joseph   74
Justice, Ralph   73

K

Kees, Phillip   74
Keller, Bruce   74
Keller, Christopher   74
Keller, Gregory   83
Keller, Harpel   74
Kellog, Elijah   74
Kellogg, Jason   74
Kelly, Henry   74
Kemmerer, Jacob   74
Kemper, Tillman   74
Kent, Absalom, Ens.   75
Kent Jr., Cephas   75
Kent, Thomas   75
Ketcham, Joshua   75
Keyser, Gary   122
Kibbe, Moses   75
Kilgore, Patrick   75
Kimball, Aaron   75
Kimball, Abraham   74
Kimmel, Nicholas   75
King, Amos   75
King, Eugene   87
King, Herman   75
King, John   75
Kingsella, David   135

Kizer, Charles   75
Kline, Lorentz, Pvt.   75
Klock, George   75, 76
Klock, George G.   76
Klotz, Johann Leonhard   76
Knight, Samuel   76
Knox, Geoffrey   50
Knox, John, Lt.   76
Koiner, George   76
Kroesen, Isaac, Pvt.   76
Krom, John   76
Krumbein, John   130

L

Lackland, Aaron   76
Ladd, John, Pvt.   76
Lake, Asa   76
Lake, Gershom   76
Lambird, Gene   100
Lampkin, James   76
Lance, John   76
Landis, Jacob, Pvt.   76
Land, Moses   77
Lane, Edward   77
Lane, James   77
Lane, Samuel, Pvt.   77
Lane, Tidence, Jr, Pvt.   77
Langworthy, James, Pvt.   77
Lanier, Burwell   77
Lanier, William   77
Lanning, George   22, 77, 111, 130
Lanning, John   77
Larrick, Casper   77
Larsen, Jerry   42
Lathrop, Dixwell   77
Laughman, Evelyn   23, 79, 90, 94, 130
Lawless, Augustine, Cpl.   77
Lawrence Jonathan, Pvt.   77
Lawson, John, Lt.   77
Lawson, Joseph   77
Lawson, Randolph   78

Lawton, Joseph 78
Lay, Larry 78
Layport, George, Pvt. 78
Lay, Thomas 78
Leach, Hezekiah, Pvt. 78
Leach, Nathan 78
Leach, William 78
Leach, William, Sr. Pvt. 78
Leake, Josiah, Capt. 78
Leavitt, Peter 78
Leeds, James, Sgt. 78
Lee, Thomas 78
LeFevre, Jacob 78
Leffingwell, Samuel 78
Leigh, Daniel 79
Leonard, George 79
Leonard, Patrick 79
Leonard, Samuel, QtrMstr. 79
Leonard, Valentine 79
Lewis, Jeremiah 79
Lewis, Philip 79
Lewis, Samuel 79
Lindsey, Archibald 79
Linsley, Simeon, Pvt. 79
Lippard, John 79
Lipscomb, Thomas 79
Little, Moses 79
Little, Thomas 79
Livermore, Daniel 79
Livers, Arnold 80
Livingston, James 80
Lockwood, Abraham, Capt. 80
Logan, James 80
Logue, John, Pvt. 80
Long, David, Pvt. 80
Long, John, 80
Long, Joseph, Pvt. 80
Long Sr., William 80
Loomis, John, Ens. 80
Looney, Peter 80
Loop, Curtis 107
Loop, Derek 107
Loop, Levi 107

Lounsbury, Michael, Pvt. 80
Lovewell, Nehemiah, Sr., Capt. 80
Loving, Gabriel, Lt. 80
Lovins, Arthur 80
Lowther, William 81
Lucas, William, Capt. 81
Ludlam, William 81
Lyman, Benjamin, Pvt. 81
Lyman, John 81
Lynch, Henry 79
Lyon, Israel , CS 81
Lyon, James, LtCol. 81
Lyon, John, Lt. 78

M

Mabie, Harmanus, Capt. 81
Mack, Betty 38, 79, 101
Maclin, Frederick, Col. 81
Macomber, Abiel, Lt. 81
Macomber, John 81
Mahan, James, Pvt. 82
Mahan, John, Lt. 82
Maine, Jonas, Ens. 82
Majors, George 82
Mammen, Christian 105
Mammen, Donald 105
Mann, Andrew, Capt. 82
Mann, Frederick 82
Mann, James 82
Manville, Nicholas 82
Maples, William Condra 82
Markham, Daniel, Pvt. 82
Marshall, Aaron, Pvt. 82
Marshall, Ezekiel 82
Marshall, Isaac 82
Marsh, Joseph , Pvt. 82
Marsteller, Philip, Lt. Col. 82
Martin, Charles 50
Martin, Isaac 83
Martin, Jacob 83
Martin, James 38
Martin, John, Lt. 83

Martin, Joseph   50, 83
Mason, George   83
Mason, Michael   40
Massia, William   83
Matheny, Christopher   60
Matthews, Moses   83
Matthews, Reuben   83
Mattice, Conrad, Pvt.   83
Maxham, Samuel, Pvt.   83
Maxwell, John, Capt.   83
Mayfield, Henry, Pvt.   84
May, Jacob   84
Mayo, John, Pvt.   84
Mayo, Joseph, Sr.   84
Mays, Benjamin, Pvt.   84
McBee, Israel   84
McClatchey, George, Pvt.   84
McCleskey, James   84
McClintock Sr., John   84
McClintock, Tyler   25, 82, 126, 133, 134
McClintock, William   84
McConnell, George   84
McCormick, William   84
McCoy, William   84
McCullers, John, Cpt.   84
McCulloch, John, Sr.   84
McDaniel, Robert   85
McDonald, Hugh   85
McDowell, Joseph   85
McDowell, Mathew, Pvt.   85
McElnay, John   85
McGee, John   85
McGlathery, Issac   85
McGrew, Patrick   85
McGrew, William   85
McGrey, James   85
McKay, Robert, Pvt.   85
McKenny, David   85
McManus, John, Pvt.   85
McNamee, Hugh   85
McNeely, Hugh   85
McNeil, John   86

McNeil, Jonathan   86
Mcnitt, Alexander, Capt.   86
McNitt, Alexander, Capt.   86
McNitt, Daniel, Sgt.   86
McQuiston, James   86
Meacham, Samuel, Pvt.   86
Means, Robert   86
Meeker, Joseph   86
Meisenheimer, Brian   86
Meisenheimer, Dean   86
Meisenheimer, Douglas   86
Meisenheimer, Patrick   86
Meisenheimer, Peter   85
Meisenheimer, Ricky   86
Meisenheimer, Willis   32, 86
Mellen, Thomas, Pvt.   86
Melson, Daniel   86
Melvin, Eugene   74
Melvin, Jonathan, Pvt.   86
Melvin, Michael   74
Melvin, William Pvt.   82
Mems, David   86
Mendenhall, Mordecai   87
Mercer, Peter   87
Mercer, Thomas   87
Meredith, John Wheeler   87
Merrifield Sr, Samuel   87
Merril, Asher   87
Merriman, Amos   87
Merriman, Elisaph   87
Merriman, Frederick   87
Meyers, Henry   87
Michener, Mordecai   87
Mickey, Daniel, Pvt.   87
Miles, Thomas, Lt.   87
Miley, John Henry   87
Miller, Benjamin, Pvt.   87
Miller, Friedrick   88
Miller, Henry, Sgt.   88
Miller, John   88
Miller Jr., James   88
Milliken, Samuel   87
Mills, Teddy   27

Ming, Wolrich 88
Minnich, Wendel 88
Mitchell, Abraham, Pvt. 88
Mitchell, David 88
Mitchell Sr., John 88
Mitchell, William 88
Moffat, Joseph, MD 88
Monk, Elias 88
Monk, William 88
Monnett, Abraham 88
Moore, Abraham 89
Moore, Andrew 89
Moore, Jonah 89
Moore, Samuel 89
Moore Sr., Jonathan 89
Moore, Thomas Guthrie, Pvt. 89
Morgan, Christopher, Ens. 89
Morgan, Solomon 89
Morgan, Temperance 89
Morgan, William 89
Morley, John 89
Morral, Samuel 89
Morrill, Abraham 89
Morrill, Ezekiel 89
Morrison, John , Sr. 90
Morris, Richard 89
Morse, Peter 90
Moser Sr., Burkhart 90
Mosher, Tobias, Pvt. 90
Moss (Morse), Joseph 90
Moss, Titus 89
Motsinger (Matzinger), Felix 90
Moulton, Daniel 90
Mount, Humphrey, Pvt. 90
Mouser/Musser, John 90
Mudge, John 90
Mulkey, Jonathan 90
Mulkey, Phillip, II 90
Mulvey, Merilee 21
Munger, Jonathan, Cpl. 90
Munger, Nathan 90
Munn, James 91

Murray, Peter 36
Murray, William 36
Musser Sr., John 91
Muzzey, John 91
Myers, Christopher, Pvt. 91
Myers, George, Pvt. 91
Myers, Henry, Ensign 90
Myers, Michael 91

N

Nakahara, Kenneth 50
Nakahara, Michael 50
Nantz, Ruben 91
Nave, Abraham, Pvt. 91
Nave, Teter 91
Nelson, Gregory 124
Nelson, Henry 91
Nelson, John 91
Nelson, Josiah 91
Nelson, Nathaniel 91
Neufang, Balthaser 92
Newhard, Michael, Sen. 92
Newman, Nimrod 92
Newton, James, Pvt. 92
Nichols, Moses 92
Nickell, Andrew 92
Noble, Stephen 92
Nonemacher, Ludwig 92
Norton, Nathan, Sgt. 92
Noyes, Bela 92
Nurse, Joseph, Pvt. 92
Nutt, James 92
Nye, David, Pvt. 92

O

Oberly, John Michael 92
Odell, John 93
Odom, John 93
Oglesby, Jessie 93
O'Hanlon, Paul 64
Ohlen, Henry George, Sgt. 93
Olin, Caleb, Ens. 93
Oliver, John 93

Olney, Joseph, Capt.   93
O'Neil, Shawn   48, 73
Oregon DAR Daughter   18, 19,
    20, 21, 22, 23, 24, 25, 26,
    27, 29, 30, 31, 32, 33, 34,
    35, 36, 37, 38, 39, 40, 41,
    42, 43, 44, 45, 46, 47, 48,
    49, 50, 51, 52, 53, 54, 55,
    56, 57, 58, 59, 60, 61, 62,
    63, 64, 65, 66, 67, 68, 69,
    70, 71, 72, 73, 74, 75, 76,
    77, 78, 79, 80, 81, 82, 83,
    84, 85, 86, 87, 88, 89, 90,
    91, 92, 93, 94, 98, 99, 100,
    101, 103, 104, 105, 107,
    108, 109, 110, 111, 112,
    113, 114, 115, 116, 117,
    118, 119, 120, 121, 122,
    123, 124, 125, 126, 127,
    128, 129, 130, 131, 132,
    133, 134, 135, 136, 137
Overacker, Adam   93
Overacker, Michael   93
Owen, David, Pvt.   93
Owen, Thomas   93

P

Packard, Robert   93
Packer, Eli   93
Page, Robert, Pvt.   93
Paine, Solomon   94
Paisley, Thomas   94
Palmer, John   94
Palmer, Rufus   94
Parish, William   94
Park, Aaron   94
Parker, Benjamin   94
Parker, Cleve   94
Parker, Eliada   94
Parker, Elisha, Pvt.   94
Parker, Gabriel   94
Parker, Henry   94
Parker, Matthew   94

Parker, Timothy   94
Parkhurst, Moses, Pvt.   93
Parkman, Henry, Jr.,
    Wagoneer   98
Park, Thomas, Cpl.   94
Parmenter, ?   98
Parmenter, Isaac, Pvt.   98
Parmenter, Jedediah   98
Parmenter, Joshua   98
Parrish, Henry   98
Parr Sr., John   98
Parsons, Joel   98
Partridge, Elisha   98
Patterson, John   98
Patterson, Robert   98
Patton, Joseph   98
Pearsall, Sampson   98
Pease, Ezekiel   99
Peck, Abel   99
Peck, Ehpraim   99
Peck, George, Pvt.   99
Peckham, Jonathan, Pvt.   99
Pedigo, Edward   99
Pemberton, Patrick Grant   99
Pence, Henry   99
Peninger, Henry   99
Penney, John, Pvt.   99
Penniman, Peter   99
Pennypack, William, Pvt.   99
Perez, Brett   38
Perez, Brian   38
Perkins, Thomas   99
Perley, Asa   99
Perley, Dudley, Lt.   99
Peters Sr., Casper   100
Phelps, Norman   100
Phillips, Asa, Pvt.   100
Phillips, Esquire, Pvt.   100
Phillips, Lot, Pvt.   100
Phillips, William   66
Phillis, Joseph   , Pvt.   100
Phipps, Samuel, Pvt.   100
Pickens, Robert Mason   100

Pickle, Mathias   98
Pierce, Caleb, NonCom   100
Pierce, James   100
Pierpont, Evelyn, Lt.   100
Pinneo, James, Capt.   100
Pinneo, Joseph, Pvt.   100
Pinney, Frances   100
Pippen, John   101
Pirkle, John Jacob   101
Pitman, Jonathan   101
Plaisted, Samuel   101
Polk, Charles   101
Polk, Charles, Capt.   101
Pollock, John, Pvt.   101
Pomeroy, Daniel, Pvt.   101
Pool Jr, Samuel   101
Poorman, Daniel, Pvt.   101
Pope, Christopher   101
Porter, Elizabeth Dunkin   101
Porter, Hugh   101
Porter, Moses   101
Porter, William, Lt. Col   101
Potter, Amos   103
Potter, Russell   103
Potter, Thomas   103
Potts, William   103
Powell, Joseph Pvt.   103
Powell, Levin   103
Powell, Moses, Pvt.   103
Powell, William, Pvt.   103
Powers, Gideon   103
Prater, Zachariah   103
Prather, Thomas, Pvt.   103
Prescott, Jedediah   103
Prescott, Timothy   104
Price, D.   104
Price, Samuel   104
Price, Stephen   34
Price, William , Jr. 1st Lt.   98
Proud, Sue   40, 94
Pruyn, Francis   104
Puckett, Drury Pvt.   104
Pullen, Stephen   104
Pulsipher, David   104
Putnam, Israel   104
Putnam, Phineas   104

Q

Quinton, Samuel   104

R

Ragland, Benjamin   104
Ramey, James, Pvt.   104, 105
Ramey Jr., Jacob   104
Ramey, Sr., Jacob   104
Rankin, James, Pvt.   105
Ransom, Samuel   105
Raviolo, John   39
Rawson, Silas   105
Ray, Andrew   105
Rayl. Samuel   104
Raymer, Frederick   105
Ray, Samuel   105
Reagan, Charles   105
Record, Josiah, Capt.   105
Record, Seth   105
Redfearn, John   105
Redman, Benjamin Pvt.   105
Redus, James, Pvt.   107
Reed, Elnathan   107
Reed, Jeremiah   107
Reed, John, Capt.   107
Reed, Joseph   107
Reed, Joshua   107
Reed, Joshua, Pvt.   107
Reitlehover, George
  Michael   107
Rench, Joseph   107
Renfrew, Mark   107
Requa, Glade   107
Reuben, Cook   108
Reynolds, Stephen   108
Rhodes, James   108
Rice, Nicholas   108
Richardson, Isaac, Pvt.   108
Richardson, Moses   108

Rickabaugh, Adam 108
Rickard, Abner 108
Rife, Jacob, Pvt. 108
Riggs, Edmond 108
Riggs, James, Pvt. 108
Riggs, Jeremiah Ellis 108
Riley, Ninian 108
Ringo, Cornelius 108
Ringo, Robert 108
Ritchie, Francis 108
Ritter, Martin 109
Robbins, Brintnal, Ens. 109
Robbins, William, Pvt. 109
Robb, James 109
Roberts, Edward 109
Roberts, Jane 109
Roberts, John 109
Robertson, Daniel, Pvt. 109
Robertson, George 109
Robertson, Mark 18
Robertson, Richard 109
Roberts, Owen Maurice 109
Roberts, Owen Maurice, Col. 109
Roberts, Richard Brook 109
Robinson, Donald 21
Robinson, John, Pvt. 109
Robison, James 109
Rodebaugh, John 110
Rodman, Joseph, Pvt. 110
Rogers, Benjamin 110
Rogers, George 39
Rogers, Josiah, Pvt. 110
Rogers, Lemuel 110
Rogers, Michael 39
Rose, Lemuel 110
Rose, Timothy, Pvt. 110
Roth, Jonathan 110
Roundy, Uriah, Pvt. 110
Rouse, Simeon, Pvt. 110
Roush, George, Pvt. 110
Rozier, Reuben 110
Ruch, Lorentz , Pvt. 110

Ruggles, Lemuel, Pvt. 110
Rugh, John Peter, Maj. 110
Rupert, Nathan 72
Russell, Andrew 111
Russell, George 111
Russell, Seth 111
Rust, Gersham, Sgt. 111
Rutledge, Edward 108
Ruyle, Henry 111
Ryland, John 111

S

Salbeda, Eric 101
Salbeda, Ian 101
Salbeda, Kade 101
Salyer, Zacheus, Pvt. 111
Sampson, Jacob 111
Sams, Jonas 111
Sandes, Henry Pvt. 111
Sanford, Ezra 111
Sanford, Oliver 111
Santee, Valentine 111
Sargent, Diamond, Pvt. 112
Sass, Donald 126, 128
Savage, James 112
Savitz, George 112
Sawin, Ezekiel, pvt. 112
Sawyer, Aaron 112
Sawyer, Benjamin 112
Sawyer, Enoch 112
Schaeffer, Anthony, Pvt. 112
Schell, Johannes Casper 112
Schenck, John, Capt. 112
Schleppi, Johannes 112
Schock, John, Pvt. 112
Schuck, Phillip 112
Schwartz, George 112
Scothorn, Elizabeth Brown 112
Scott, James, Lt. 113
Scott, John 113
Scott, Richard 24
Scott, Thomas 113
Scranton, Timothy, Pvt. 113

Scribner, Levi 113
Scroggins, Humphrey 113
Seamans, Hezekiah, Pvt. 113
Sears, Nathan 113
Sears, Richard, Sgt. 113
Seaver, Daniel, Pvt. 113
Seaver, Moses, Pvt. 113
Seeber, Saffreness 113
Seitz, Peter 113
Selkirk, James, Sgt. 113
Seltzer, Jacob 113
Seltzer, Michael, Pvt. 114
Settle, Reuben 114
Sevier, John, Col. 114
Seymour, Aaron 114
Shackelford, Henry 114
Shaklee, Peter, Pvt. 114
Shakro, Wilbur 40
Shallenberger, John 114
Shanks, Thomas 114
Sharp, Isaac 114
Sharp, Jacob, Pvt. 114
Shattuck, Job, Capt. 114
Shattuck, Sarah Hartwell 114
Shears, Andrew 114
Sheldon, James 112
Sheldon Sr., James 114
Shelly, Daniel, Pvt. 112
Shepard, Elisha 115
Shepard, James 115
Shepard, Robert 115
Shepardson, John 115
Shepard, Timothy 115
Sheppard, Charlton 115
Sherman, Eber 115
Sherman, John, Sr. 115
Sherman, Rodger 115
Sherwood, Abel 115
Shields, William, Capt. 115
Shipman, Abraham 115
Shive, George 115
Shoemaker, David 74
Shoemaker, John George, Pvt. 115

Shuford, John 116
Sill, Jabez, Jr., Pvt. 116
Simmons, Frederick 116
Simons, Adriel 116
Singleton, Richard, Pvt. 116
Skelton, John, Ensign 111
Skidmore, James 116
Skidmore, John, Cpt. 116
Skinner, Eli 116
Slade, Peleg, LtCol. 116
Slaughter Sr., Owen 116
Small, Elisha Edward 116
Small, Matthew 116
Small, Micah 116
Smith, Anderson 116
Smith, Brandon 75
Smith, Cameron 75
Smith, Downing Rucker 117
Smith, Edward 117
Smith, Henry 117
Smith, Israel, Capt. 117
Smith, Jacob, Pvt. 117
Smith, Jeffrey 74
Smith, Joseph 117
Smith, Moses 117
Smith, Nathan 117
Snow, Bernice 117
Snow, John 117
Snow, Samuel 117
Snow, Thomas 117
Soblet (Sublett), Benjamin, Cpl. 117
Sollers, Thomas, Maj. 117
Soule, James 117
Southmayd, William, Sgt. 118
Sowers, Paul 118
Spear, Jonathan, Cpt. 118
Spears, Christian 118
Spears, George F., Pvt. 118
Spencer, Elam, Pvt. 118
Spiegel, John 31
Sprague, Hezekiah 118
Sprankel, Michael 118
Sprankel, Peter, Sr 118

Springermann, Clayton   114
Springermann, Travis   114
Springer, Philip   118
Sproul, Robert   118
Sproul, William   118
Spurgeon/Spurgin, James   118
Stackhouse, John, Pvt.   118
Standish, Shadrack, Drm.   118
Stanford, Moses Pvt   119
Stanford, Richard, Pvt.   119
Staples, Isaac, Pvt.   119
Staples, Nathaniel, Pvt.   119
Starbuck, Matthew   119
Stark Sr., Daniel   119
Starkweather, John, Sgt   119
Starling, Adam   119
Stearns, Levi, Sgt.   119
Stearns, Peter   119
Steckel, Peter   119
Steele, Bradford, Sr., Capt.   119
Steele Sr., Bradford, Capt.   119
Stemple, Godfrey   119
Stephens, Gilbert, Pvt.   119
Stevens, Joseph, Cpl.   119
Stevenson, James   120
Stevens, Thomas, Pvt.   120
Stewart, Alexander, Pvt.   120
Stewart, John   120
Stewart, Robert   93
Stewart Sr., John   120
Stocker, Andreas, Pvt.   120
Stockwell, David   120
Stoddard, David   120
Stolp, Peter   120
Stone, Anthony   120
Stone, John, Pvt.   120
Stone, Moses, Jr.   120
Stoner, David   120
Stotts, Solomon   120
Stow, Elihu, Jr., Pvt.   120
Stowell, David   120
Strawn, Isaiah   121
Strawn, Jacob   121

Strong, Josiah, Pvt.   121
Sturtevant, Jesse, Lt.   121
Sublett, Benjamin, Cpl.   121
Sutherland, William   121
Sutton, John B., Pvt.   121
Sweetser, John, Lt.   121
Sweet, Sylvester   121
Swift, Flower   121
Swigert, Philip, Pvt.   121
Swim, Roger   75
Szolomayer, Gary   87

𝒯

Taft, Caleb   121
Taliferro, Craig   121
Tanner, George   104
Tavenner, George   121
Taylor Sr., Othniel   122
Temple, Joseph, Pvt.   122
Temple, Solomon   122
Tenney, John, Pvt.   122
Terrell, Edmund, Capt.   122
Terrell, Josiah, Capt.   122
Terry, Parshall, Pvt.   122
Thomas, Alexander   122
Thomas, Charles   136
Thomas, Don   90
Thomas, Patrick   136
Thomas, Simon   122
Thomas, William   122
Thompson, Benajah   123
Thompson, Charles   53
Thompson, Robert   123
Thompson, Samuel   123
Thompson, Thaddeus, Pvt.   123
Thrash, Valentine   123
Threlkeld, John, Pvt.   123
Thurston, David, Pvt.   123
Ticknor, Daniel   123
Tieman, Connor   95
Tieman, Michael   2, 94
Tieman-Woodward, Owen   95
Tilghman, Joshua   123

Tiller, John   123
Tilley, Lazarus   123
Tillson, William, Pvt   123
Timmons, Nehemiah   123
Tindall, William   123
Tinder, James   122
Tingley, Lemuel   124
Tipps, Jacob   124
Todd, Jonah   124
Tofflemire, Martin   124
Tolman, Benjamin   124
Tompkins, Gideon, Pvt.   124
Tower, Nathaniel, Cpl.   124
Trickey Sr., John   124
Trimble, James   124
Troutman, John   124
Trowbridge, Edmund, Sgt.   124
Troxell, Daniel, Pvt.   124
Troxell, Peter, Sr.   124
Trumbell, David   124
Tubbes, George   124
Tucker, Ephraim   125
Tucker, John, Pvt.   125
Tune, Travis   125
Turner, Kerenhappuch   125
Turner, Meshack   125
Turner, William, Pvt.   125
Turney, Adam, Ens.   125
Tuthill, Samuel   125
Tuttle, Sylvanus   125
Tyler, Samuel   125

U

Underhill, Israel   125
Underhill, John   125
Utter, Abraham, Pvt.   125

V

Vance, Patrick   126
Van Cleave, Benjamin   126
Van Deusen, Matthew, Cpl.   126
Van Meter, Jacob   126
Van Meter Sr, Jacob   126

Van Ness, Peter   126
Vannosdall, Oakey, Pvt.   126
Van Slyke, Harmanus   126
Van Tassel, Abraham   126
Van Wormer, Jacob, Lt.   126
Varnes (Werns; Werntz), George, Ens.   126
Vars, Isaac   126
Veeder, Volkert   126
Venable, Charles   126
Verigan, Neil   105
Vernon, Richard, Capt.   127
Vernon, Richard, PS   127

W

Waddell, Samuel   33
Wagensailer, John, Pvt.   127
Wagner, Jesston   79
Wainscott, Abraham   127
Waitman-Ingebretsen, Patti   30, 43, 47, 53, 63, 76, 83, 88, 91, 105, 116, 133, 134
Walden Sr., Richard   127
Waldron, Peter   127
Walker, John, Sgt.   127
Walker, Sr., John   127
Wallace, Josiah   127
Waller, Benjamin   127
Walls, George   128
Waltman Jr., Conrad   127
Wampler Sr., George   127
Ward, David   128
Ward, John, Pvt.   127
Ware, Samuel   131
Ware, William, Pvt.   127
Warlick, Barbara   128
Warner, Eliphaz   128
Warner, Jonathan, Lt.   128
Warner, Nathan, Cpl.   128
Warner, Nathaniel   128
Warner, William   128
Warren, Caleb Dennis   128
Warren, Gideon   128

Warren, Martin, Pvt.   128
Washburn, Joseph   128
Washburn, Joseph, Pvt.   128
Washington, John
   Augustine   128
Waterman, Sr, Daniel, Pvt.   129
Waters, Steven   135
Watkins, Evan   129
Watkins, Nathan, Capt.   129
Watts, Nicholas   129
Waugh, John, Pvt.   129
Wear, Donald   128
Weaver, Samuel   129
Weaver, Samuel J.   129
Webber, Bradley   129
Webb, Solon   74
Webster, Jonathan   129
Webster Sr., Constant   129
Weed, Eleazer, Pvt.   129
Weed, Gilbert, Pvt.   129
Weed Jr, John   129
Weeks, Phillip, Pvt.   129
Weidner, Heinrich   129
Wells, Joseph, Maj.   130
Wells, Shaylor, Pvt.   130
Wentz, Johan Jost   130
West, Thomas   130
Wetzel, Adama   130
Whaley, James, Jr., 2nd Lt.   130
Whaley, James, Sr.   130
Whealdon, Isaac   127
Wheat, Thomas   130
Wheeler, Peter, Pvt.   130
Wheeler Sr, Aaron   130
Whicker, James   130
Whitaker, Joseph   130
Whitaker, Joshua   130
White, John   130
White, John, Pvt.   131
White, Joseph, Pvt.   131
Whitener, Henry, Jr.   131
Whitener Jr, Henry   131
White, Thomas   130, 131
White, Thompson   131
White, William   131
Whitmarsh, Jacob   131
Whitner Jr, Henry   131
Whitney, Joshua, Sgt.   131
Whitney, William, Pvt.   131
Whitsitt, William Wirt
   Whiteside   131
Whittier, Daniel   131
Whittier, Robert   131
Whittington, Issac   131
Whittlesey Jr., Eliphalet,
   Pvt.   131
Wicker, Robert   131
Wickizer, Conrad   132
Wiest, Earl   104
Wight, Bennett   132
Wilder, Thomas   132
Wilhoit, Jesse   132
Wilkins, James   132
Willett, George   132
Willett, Grace   132
Willey, Absalom   132
William Porter, Lt. Col.   132
Williams, Benjamin   132
Williams, Christopher   74
Williams, Daniel, Capt.   132
Williams, Hardin   132
Williams, Israel   132
Williams, James   132
Williams, John   132
Williams, Joseph   128
Willis, Stoughton   132
Willson, Nahum   133
Wilson, Andrew, Pvt.   133
Wilson, Christopher   81
Wilson, Connor   81
Wilson, James   132
Wilson, Jessie   133
Wilson, Matthew, Pvt.   133
Wilson, Robert   133
Wilson, William, Pvt.   133
Winans, Lewis   133

Winckelbleck, John Adam 133
Winslow, Ezra 133
Winsor, Henry 115
Witherspoon, John 133
Witt, Elisha, Pvt. 133
Wixom, John 133
Wixom, Peleg 133
Wolcott, Gideon, Sgt. 134
Womack, Abraham 134
Wood, Jeremiah, Pvt. 134
Woodmansee, James, Lt. 134
Woods, Abija 134
Woods, Adam, Sgt. 134
Woods, Hugh 134
Woods, John 134
Woods, Samuel, Pvt. 134
Woods, Solomon, Lt. 134
Woods, Susannah Wallace 134
Woodworth, Gershom 134
Wooldridge, Richard 134
Woolverton, Daniel 134
Word, Charles 134
Worden, Joseph 135
Worden, Nathaniel 135
Workman, Jacob 135
Wright, Benjamin 135
Wright, Elisha, Cpl. 135
Wright, Isaac 135
Wright, Ithamar 135
Wright, Robert 135
Wright Sr., Richard 135
Wright, Stephen, Pvt. 130
Wyatt, Joshua 136

Y

Yandle, James 136
Yaple, Jacob, Pvt. 136
Yaple, Phillip H. 136
Yeager, John 136
Yeager Sr., Adam 136
Yeasley, George 136
Yerkes, James, Pvt. 136
Young, Elkanah 136
Young, Ivon 112
Young, Jacob 136
Young, John, Pvt. 136

Z

Zachary, James, Pvt. 136
Zehner, Adam 136
Zimmerman, George 137
Zumwalt, Adam 137
Zumwalt, Christopher 137
Zumwalt, Jacob 137

www.ingramcontent.com/pod-product-compliance
Lightning Source LLC
Chambersburg PA
CBHW041612220426
43669CB00001B/8